YOUR MONEY COUNTS

A STEP-BY-STEP APPROACH TO DISCOVERING BIBLICAL FINANCIAL FREEDOM

MARK LLOYDBOTTOM

WITH HOWARD DAYTON

CROWN FINANCIAL MINISTRIES
biblical financial freedom

Crownuk.org

With thanks to the Crown Financial Ministries Gainesville team, so many of whom supported and encouraged Rhoda and I as we followed God's calling to introduce the Crown Financial Ministries' study programmes to the UK and Ireland. We thank God for your commitment to sharing your books and study resources not only with us, but also with all other countries. I thank Crown in the US for their willingness to allow us to adapt the books to include our own experiences and understanding of what I have learnt not only in the church, but also as a professional and author on business, financial and tax planning.

My thanks to Howard Dayton, the original author for the many hours he allowed me to spend with him drawing from his experience and understanding of God's Word regarding how we can better manage our money, wealth and possessions.

My thanks also to all those who have helped me publish this version. There are many and to all of them I am grateful. I would particularly like to thank Gillian Searle and Steven Pierce for their editing expertise, Peter Briscoe, Crown's European vice president and finally Fleur Isbell, my typesetter, to all of them my thanks.

Mark Lloydbottom

Contents

one
Fifteen thousand and counting

I returned home after playing football at school – I was drenched from the downpour a few minutes earlier as I squelched up to the front door. I had scored a couple of good goals, but missed some sitters. My shoes were soaked and scuffed and I knew that my mother would have something to say as they were less than a week old. I rang the doorbell to our flat, but there was no reply. That meant mum was late returning from work and with my brother staying on at chess club I knew I would be alone for some time. I found the key hidden under the stone by the dustbin and let myself in as I always did twice a week. I was destined never to forget that day.

As I entered our living room I looked at the television and wondered if it was time to watch Andy Pandy – a programme that always seemed entertaining but by today's standards definitely even beyond old fashioned. After Andy Pandy I would watch Blue Peter with Christopher Trace and Lelia Williams. With ten minutes before it was time to switch on the black and white Bush television I sat and stared around the room. My eyes glanced onto a pile of papers and I got up with my wet socks still hugging my feet and approached the table with a measure of curiosity. I looked and wanted to take a peek – my first recollection of being nosey.

Mum's weekly letter from gran, a form from the Inland Revenue, a few of her exquisitely handwritten notes and then I saw a bank statement. What was this I wondered? I recall seeing mum along with others go into 'my bank' and I had begun to work out some aspects of how our home finances worked, but this was the first bank statement I had ever seen. I looked intensely; debit, credit – what did those words mean? In the credit column there was an entry that had my dad's initials alongside. I had never really known any parent other than my mum; others had a dad, but not me. I later discovered that they had separated five years earlier. My eyes were drawn toward the final column. This was headed 'balance' and even as a seven year old that was a word I instinctively comprehended.

Thirteen pounds ten shillings – is that *all* we have left to live on? I was gripped with worry as I asked myself 'how are we going to survive?'

Suddenly, I heard the key turning in the lock and realised that mum was home so I hurriedly collected the papers and replaced them how I had found them a few moments earlier. I raced over to the television and turned the set on – by the time mum came in the screen was 'warming up' and the familiar signature tune of Blue Peter could be heard as the sea and ship became clearer on the ever glowing screen. What about Andy Pandy I thought? I realised how long I had been looking at the bank statement, what I thought it showed and what I perceived was our perilous financial situation. I had little interest in Christopher Trace's models, not even the ones he had made earlier, for all I could think about was my discovery that mum had little or no money and we were in trouble.

Early learning

Thus my childhood was partly framed by knowing there was no money other than for basics. How did finance flow into the household? Well, I worked out that it only trickled and came from mum's job as a receptionist at a dental practice, my absent father and gifts from my uncle. The home finances did not allow for anything other than the basics of food, clothes and shelter. Clothing? I always looked forward to mum taking me shopping for clothes. The 'Nearly New' shop in Wolverhampton supplied our household with just about everything we required. Eating out? Occasionally, mum would take me out to one of two Chinese restaurants that had recently opened, although those outings ceased when the local newspaper reported that one of those restaurants was accused of killing cats and serving them as chicken.

No matter how challenging mum found her finances, I later realised how carefully she had managed. Her stewardship enabled us to move from the flat she rented to a house. She told me she now had a mortgage, a term I did not understand.

Like any youngster I wanted to be able to spend – sweets and superman comics were top of my list. At the age of eight I joined the local church choir where, provided I attended practice on Fridays and both Sunday services, I could earn nine (old) pence. We were paid quarterly and so I looked forward to the choir master giving me my brown envelope containing almost ten shillings (50p). Whenever I sang at a wedding I earned 2/6d (12.5p) and sometimes there were three weddings on a Saturday, so that was a day to look forward to, especially as the pay was handed out at the end of the wedding service, almost as soon as the last guest had left to join the photo call.

Teen lessons

I looked forward with anticipation to the day when I could, like my older brother, start a newspaper round. Eventually when I came of working age, as well as delivering papers I worked on a Saturday morning at a local hotel cleaning doors, skirting boards and windows. Knowing mum had little or no money I applied myself to earning everything I could so that I could finance my desires to enjoy some of the good things in life. As a teenager I enjoyed those days in the sixties. I earned and spent money as it passed through my hands. I started to watch the local football team who in those days were in football's elite division and provided good entertainment and excitement. For my birthdays and Christmas, gran, my aunts and uncles would send me money and I would make the long haul into the town centre to the building society to add to my savings – that was money for another day.

When I reached sixteen, mum stopped receiving child support from dad and so I followed my brother's path in leaving school – and leaving behind those who progressed to higher education. It was time to train, and earn and contribute to the household budget.

Time for work

My first interview was with Chubb, whose business had started in Wolverhampton in 1820 and is now a global enterprise. I was 17 and had never before been interviewed. My next interview was with an insurance company: "What is the purpose of insurance?" I could not answer, but I do recall being told that the right answer was 'using the money of the fortunate to help those who are not so fortunate.' Next I sat opposite a bank manager. I noticed his well furnished office, and as he sat behind his large desk with a broad smile I looked up and tried to be as composed as I could. I had been accustomed to teachers, been afraid of the headmaster and deputy head, but was not used to being interviewed for a job. Mum suggested I give my father a call. So I called dad and told him about my interview experiences and he told me that with the jobs I had applied for I would be waiting for 'dead men's shoes.' Three interviews and no job offer – I was on a steep learning curve and in need of an employer.

I returned to the Youth Employment Bureau, the office which back in the sixties was charged with providing assistance to help school leavers get into the job market. I recounted my experiences to Mr Mills, the chief Youth Employment Officer, and after completing some tests was advised to go and have an interview with an accountant. My brother was an articled clerk and studying to be a chartered accountant and so I knew that this required a lot of studying, but at the end of the rainbow I would be able to earn abundantly. This interview was different. I was talking to Malcolm Gilbert who was the liaison officer for all accountancy firms in Wolverhampton. He was responsible for interviewing prospective trainees and then reassigning their applications to other firms. "I would like to offer you a job." Those words were music to my ears. I was there, on my way – now I would be able to go to all the home games and maybe even some away ones, as well as being able to buy some trendy clothes.

Training to be an accountant

I started my training in Wolverhampton and having passed my first two professional exams in double quick time, I decided to take advantage of an Institute of Chartered Accountants scheme allowing me to take a training break and spend six months working in industry. At the age of 20 I left home and drove my Morris Minor estate to Southampton where I had a room booked at the YMCA and a job in 'fixed assets' at a synthetic rubber company. I knew what fixed assets were, but why would it need a whole department?

Shortly after starting there I was called into the chief accountant's office, "Will you go and work on the production line? Your salary will continue and we will pay you for working on the line." This was the early seventies and strikes were commonplace. The workers at the Hythe plant had gone on strike for more pay while the syndicate of rubber company owners were demanding that production continue. I had doubled my salary during these six months in industry and now it was going to quadruple. On my first day as a manual worker I approached the factory entrance in my car. Ahead of my gleaming bonnet I could see a lot of people milling around the factory gate. As I drew closer I saw police jostling with strikers, whose job I was about to undertake. I slowed down and drove slowly through the turbulent mass of bodies. I was used to being part of a swaying crowd at football, but never one as angry as this. I drove through the picket line accompanied by a cacophony of shouting. As I parked with the noise echoing in the distance, I looked at my car. I had bought it from a friend who had looked after it with great care for over 70,000 miles, but now there were cigarette burns all down the sides. I realised I had crossed a line that some thought was not mine to traverse and they used their cigarettes to show their disapproval.

That evening I watched the local news and saw the reports from outside the factory gate. Strikes were almost inevitably about more pay and this one was no exception as workers demanded a pay increase of 15%. That evening I reflected; never did I imagine that I would be a 'scab.' Why should I, after all I had decided to train to become an accountant!

We were all instructed to meet at the company's Southampton offices the next day as arrangements had been made to transfer us to the Hythe plant. As the minibus with its ten occupants approached the gates we could see TV cameras, police and a seething mass of workers. As we slowly passed down the picket line the minibus was rocked from side to side as the strikers let us know they vehemently disapproved of what we were doing. Angry faces were centimetres from the window as they banged on the glass and shouted, 'scab, scab.' I was probably more frightened that day than the previous one. The police were outnumbered and unable to hold back the line of fire that was directed toward those who had dared to accept management's request to 'keep the plant' going.

I headed toward the synthetic rubber production line and the coagulation tanks for another day of watching rubber bales pass by. I reflected about those on the picket line I had just passed through, their commitment to the cause for increased pay and their anger as we had broken through their line. I reflected on how important money was to them as well as to me. I had accepted the opportunity because it seemed like an adventure and a way to make money. I had little time to contemplate further as the foreman, Mr Wood, a towering man also known as 'timber,' entered the canteen to bark out instructions. He was a man I instantly learned to respect and obey; his presence was commanding as he sought to show the white collar staff how to keep the bales moving. I looked at the dark yellow bales and wondered what happened to them after they left the plant – how did they become tyres?

Finding my wife

At Above Bar Church in Southampton I met Rhoda, a woman to whom I was immediately attracted. She was recently divorced and had a young baby, Philip. We married within a year and settled down. At the end of six months I found a new employer who agreed to continue my training contract. The salary remained low and I struggled to provide my new family with anything but the basics. Now I had a wife and child to provide for, but we had both been used to living on low incomes and so were well prepared. Little did our next door neighbours know that when they offered us food from their garden or their store cupboard we barely had enough for our next meal. Our shopping was supplemented by luncheon vouchers which were given to me as a perk. Tough times? Yes, to us they were, but we were happy and totally in love – little else really mattered.

Preparing accounts in Bristol

After qualifying we moved to Bristol and I found an accountancy firm looking to employ staff who had qualified with a national firm.

"Come and see me please Mark." As I entered the partners' office he greeted me and asked me to take a seat. "At your interview you asked not to prepare any more farm accounts" (I worked on farm accounts in Wolverhampton and found that farmers' records were often very incomplete). I would like you to go to….The following Monday I drove to the farm in south Bristol to start work on preparing six years' worth of accounts. I was greeted by the farmer's wife and introduced to the family. Soon I was sitting in an 'office' in the farmhouse loft. I looked around and found post that hadn't been opened for six years – hundreds of unopened envelopes!

I was invited to join the family for lunch. The farmer's wife and son chatted freely while the farmer sat sullenly without uttering one word. This was a new experience for me and it felt a little uncomfortable. "How do you know which bills to pay?," I asked. It occurred to me during the four hours of opening post that they must have a different system of paying bills. "We wait until John, the bailiff comes; he tells us what to pay." "Oh, that's interesting," I responded. I had found two envelopes with out-of-date cheques. "What about cheques for the sale of cattle and crops?" I enquired. "I know what those envelopes look like" was Joan's reply. As the week passed I progressed with the accounts preparation and lunch times became a little more relaxed as the conversation widened. However the farmer did little more than grunt as he sat at the head of the table looking very morose.

By lunchtime on Friday, I could see the farm was in severe financial straits. As I opened the letters from the bank I could see the manager was concerned at the state of the finances. Over lunch, I mentioned that the farm was in deep financial straits, "Did they know?," I awkwardly enquired.

The weekend was enjoyable; we went to the park to fly kites and then shopping in the afternoon to buy the suite we had been planning to purchase for six months. We had made a lot of friends with other couples living in our avenue, it was summer and we spent the weekend socialising with our neighbours.

Monday morning and on the journey to the farm I contemplated my plans for completing the accounts. I thought of sandwiches in the office rather than lunch in the farmhouse. As I turned the corner I was confronted with flashing blue lights and as I looked ahead I could see an ambulance and three police cars. "Come in please, we would like to speak with you." As I passed through the farm I could see the family crying as they were coming to terms with finding the farmer hanging in the barn. The strain of trying to make the farm profitable had taken its toll and he had given up on solving the farm's financial problems.

Six months later the same partner called, "Come in and see me please Mark." Once I was sat in his office he said, "we have a construction company that is owned by a very astute client, he is an accountant and we need you to go and finalise the company accounts. He has prepared draft accounts which show a profit of £140,000. The bank is asking for audited figures as the cash flow is quite tight."

A week later I reported back to the partner with accounts that showed a *loss* of £120,000. "Do you know what you are doing?" The question was asked more than a little tersely. 'Yes', I said 'I know the accounts are different from the client's and I can explain why. There is a serious problem with the company's valuation of stock and work in progress – it is definitely overstated.'

Three days later, the accountant committed suicide by jumping off the Clifton suspension bridge, a favourite spot for those who seek to prematurely end their life. The accountant had been colluding with the site foreman who had been ordering construction materials and then diverting them to his house before selling them and splitting the proceeds with his lady friend, the accountant.

Starting in business

Two years later I realised my ambition to work for myself when I launched my own accountancy business. With assistance from another accountant who gave me some subcontract work, I worked as many hours for him as

I could while at the same time seeking to find my own clients. After three months I employed a part-time secretary who I knew from church and the business moved into an office.

We were soon gaining new clients as bank managers were happy to recommend the new kid on the block. As we grew, we hired staff but then there was a two-month period when we won no new clients. No matter what marketing I did or who I spoke with, the phone didn't ring with any enquiries. As Christine left at lunch time, I told her that I had been praying for new clients. I had tried everything else; why not try praying I thought. The next morning I couldn't wait for Christine to arrive so I could tell her that we had three calls and would be engaging three new clients. From that day I started to apply my faith to my business and my finances.

Budget day

Over the next twenty five years I built three businesses including a publishing company and an Internet business. The publishing company's activities included publishing Budget reports which we wrote immediately after the Chancellor's annual Budget statement. These reports were ordered by accountants to send to their clients and our role was to preprint the firm's details on the covers ready for budget day. On Budget day we would print hundreds of thousands of reports and then on the finishing lines they were collated with the preprinted covers and then despatched overnight to accountants' offices. After our first year we grew to the extent that the trimming of the covers was outsourced by our printer. If Andy, the managing director of the print company had known the trimming company would go into liquidation hours after he had delivered the covers, he would not have let his vans leave the premises.

With 24 hours to go before the Budget, the covers were behind locked doors. No matter who I contacted or what we did the factory doors remained locked. My mind was in overdrive and a state of panic as I knew that if we didn't deliver the reports we would be sued by hundreds of accountants and the business which had enjoyed a meteoric start would be doomed.

I had exhausted every avenue – we all had – by this time there were about 20 staff from our two companies outside the factory. Then, I announced to everyone that I was going to do a 'Joshua' and walk around the factory seven times and ask God to open the doors. No one who was there will ever forget that day. I walked around the factory – each circuit took about two minutes. I prayed all the way; in the state I was in, praying was easy. After six laps I knew the ultimate lap was around the corner and as I walked I prayed more earnestly than before. Everyone else sat there worried – I had gone beyond that! As I came around the corner for the seventh time a car drove up to the factory gate and stopped. The driver jumped out and said "I know what has happened to you, this is not your problem and it's not fair. I am going to open the doors for ten minutes, get your covers out – that's all the time you can have."

That left a deep impression on Andy, the managing director of the print company, and Sheila my co-director. Me? I just know I serve a God who is truly amazing and cares for us individually.

Knowing God

At the age of twelve I went on youth camp and after listening to the speaker decided to become a Christian. Life has not been the same since. There have been many tough times when my belief in God has helped me through. We live in times when many seek to ignore or ridicule God, but it is my testimony that I know God loves me and is interested in what I am doing. He is there for me when I succeed and when I fail.

This book may have been given to you by a friend; you may have acquired it from a book shop or as part of the preliminary Crown study course. I trust you will enjoy discovering how you can change your approach to finances. This book unlocks secrets for those who are rich or poor, young or old, male or female, Christian or non-Christian.

I have learnt about finances through studying and applying what I find in the Bible, putting it into practice at home and in the workplace. From poverty to financial independence; from being in debt to debt-free; from having no savings to accruing savings. I have been privileged to counsel the poor as well as the rich. What you will find in this book works – every time.

The chapter title? From the age of twelve I have learnt so much. I have shared some of the key events relating to how God prepared me for writing this book and working with Crown Financial Ministries. How long has it taken? Somewhere approaching 15,000 days, maybe more.

I have seen the consequences of dishonesty by others. The stories are real, the lessons relevant to today. Chapter two takes a look at the state of our finances as a whole.

two
What state are our finances in?

We all have memories that will last forever; maybe you have a memory from your childhood days? For some it may have been the death of Princess Diana while for others a memorable event in space. For me, it was 1966 the year when England won the football World Cup. However, a less memorable event occurred that year as it was also the year the credit card arrived in this country.

You may feel financially challenged, and probably know you are not the only one. Having described my personal journey in the preceding chapter we will look briefly at the state of personal finances across the nation, where we are and how we arrived here. Included are some numbers based on statistics and surveys, which are as up-to-date as we can make them. Since the introduction of the credit card we have gone from very little unsecured debt to a position where the average unsecured debt per household *for those who have such debt* is in excess of £21,000[1]. This exceeds the average unsecured debt (which takes every household in the country into account regardless of whether they have debt) which is now over £10,000. Furthermore, according to the Griffiths Commission the debt-to-income ratio has risen from around 40% in 1975, to just over 100% in 1995, to 140% in 2005. This is higher than in the US and most other large European countries.

Like any commercial organisation, the ultimate objective is to make a profit. And credit card companies never fail to do that.

The day our children were 18, the credit card application forms started to arrive. How attractive and seductive some of those marketing enticements looked! Offers of interest-free periods, offers of loans. Skilled marketers know how to entice prospects to become customers. When my son attended Freshers Week he was invited to have a credit card to 'make buying books and coffee easy.' On one occasion he received a letter with a cheque from a credit card company – all he had to do was bank it.

There are now more credit cards in circulation than there are people in this country.

When you buy a new game, your first task is to find the rules, read them and then follow them. The company that made the game makes up the rules for the players to follow. If you have unsecured debt does it ever feel like that to you? The lender makes up the rules – that includes the interest rate and repayment terms. They decide on the charges for late payment – you pay if you are one small step out of line with your monthly payment.

And the rate of interest they charge on your debt? Even with a low base rate, many of the credit card companies are charging interest rates of 17 percent or more. That is more than 10 percent above the bank base rate.

When I first opened a bank account every transaction was made by cheque. Today, there are probably no more than two cheque entries on any one statement. Plastic has become the primary means of exchange, not withstanding the fact there are those who only use cash. Most transactions that pass directly onto my account are made via debit card, while my credit card has an automatic direct debit payment mechanism that results in my month's purchases being charged to my bank account.

With paying being so automatic and electronic, it is easy to become detached from the outstanding debt which for so many has been increasing. Years ago banks used to use red ink to indicate an overdrawn balance – now everything is 'in the black.'

Pensioners in debt

It is easy to assume it is those approaching middle age who are most burdened with debt. While this is so, this group probably also has parents who are deep in the grip of debt. Pensioners who might have dreamed about being mortgage-free by the time they retire have combined debt of over £50 billion, leaving them trying to work out how to manage their finances on reduced income. Maybe the debt of pensioners gives some insight as to why the generations that follow have similarly become accustomed to relying on debt.

15 – 25 year olds

A survey of those aged 16 to 25 called 'Penny for your thoughts' exploring young peoples' relationships with and attitudes towards finance shows that:

- only 6% of respondents said they manage their money by sticking to a fixed budget
- two in ten (22%) said they just cross their fingers and hope they don't run out of cash

- more than two thirds (68%) of respondents had been encouraged to take out credit they either did not want or could not afford
- a third (34%) of the young people that completed the survey had debt-related problems at the time, and a further 13% had done in the past.

According to the survey, millions of teenagers are planning to fund their lifestyle through credit cards, overdrafts and loans. As many as 44% of 15 to 17 year olds are planning to take out a credit card when they become an adult; 18% are thinking of taking out a bank loan when they turn 18 and a further 17% expect to be overdrawn.

Student loans

Over three million students owe more than £25 billion in student loans with the maximum available loan now more than £25,000 before any interest is added. Many students leave higher education with student debt in excess of £15,000 and have to factor in repayments which in the early years of working often do not even cover the cost of interest.

New debt for old?

Watching daytime television I was amazed how many advertisements there were for debt consolidation loans. What do I think of consolidation loans? Personally, I dislike them intensely and in my role as an accountant and financial adviser would never recommend them. In my opinion, the clue to the real nature of these loans is in their name, CONsolidation. A CONsolidation loan pays off all unsecured debts and creates a new loan account to which you may add in some extra cash borrowing. These loans combine debts which probably have varying interest rates and term periods into one loan with one payment. Sometimes loans have a penalty clause for early repayment which is triggered on consolidation.

The net effect is normally threefold:

1. The length of time to repay is stretched, and so
2. The monthly repayments reduce, and so
3. The total interest paid increases compared to what you would have paid, and as a result

many people who consolidate their debts in this way find they have spare cash each month and start to spend it and then...the new balance on the credit card doesn't get paid off at the end of the month. The cycle of debt has begun again. In fact it is estimated that the majority of people who take out a consolidation loan actually end up in further debt.

Ways in which we are persuaded to spend money

With more than £6,000 spent on marketing for every person in this country there are always spending opportunities for us to contemplate. It would be quite easy to write a book on spending temptations, so I have decided to highlight a few that appear to be optional, unnecessary and in some cases addictive.

1. Online gambling

There are now more than 2,000 websites dedicated to online gambling. These sites often use the word gaming in order to avoid the word gambling. The offers of free gambling money are there to entice you to spend (or should I say, lose) your hard earned money. Remember, the people who make up the rules win. You only have to look at pictures of Las Vegas hotels and casinos to know that the owners of gambling establishments have the odds well and truly stacked in their favour. How addictive is online gambling? Very; the average spend per annum of those who gamble is more than £1,000. At the extreme it was reported that a 30-year old Chinese man died of exhaustion after playing games online for three days.

2. TV phone ins

Now, maybe by this point, you think I am a killjoy. Not so, but the TV companies have admitted rigging competitions so that they could profiteer from your calls. How much do you spend in a year? If you are in debt, double it to take account of the interest you could have saved by not making that call.

3. TV shopping channels

I have fleetingly watched these channels with interest although never been tempted to buy more 'stuff.' It seems that more than 80% of what they sell is only going to appeal to those who wish to buy on impulse. There is an endless focus on what the product could do for you and how you will look, accompanied by 'the saving' they offer. But, you have to spend to save.

4. Internet spending

Like the television it is so easy to click and spend. I use the Internet to buy those services that I have to buy. I cannot recall ever buying any 'stuff' as a result of website advertisements. I recall my daughter telling me she used to pay as much as £10 a month for ringtones. That is probably one reason why I decided to be careful with my own click and spend habits.

5. Watch out there are charges about

Banks and credit card companies have been taken to task regarding their practice of high charges when an account goes overdrawn or a payment is made late. I recall one newspaper story that recounted how one bank had managed to make an unauthorised overdraft of £10 into a debt of more than £350. When ordering online there are sometimes hidden charges that are only advised at the end of the transaction.

Your finances are not secure

In one two-year period my credit card was subject to fraud three times while my bank managed to resurrect a credit card account that had been closed three years previously and then charge me £80 for their 'error.' Now, with bank and credit card payment systems dominated by automatic charges, it is essential to keep track of payments on your accounts, either online or by text. There are far too many people dedicated to fraud who are seeking to access your accounts. It is almost impossible to be over-diligent, but it is very easy to miss fraudulent transactions unless you check carefully the payments charged to your accounts.

Savings

The British media regularly focus on the so-called 'pensions crisis.' The shortfall statistics are normally reported as being in the billions which, if you are like me, you switch over to working out what that means for you. We work for up to 75,000 hours in our lifetime to have the prospect of a retirement that enables us to decide what to do with our time. A reward for all that hard work? Well, that might be what some achieve, but there are a good proportion of pensioners for whom that is not the case.

How has this happened?

Those retiring today are sometimes referred to as the baby boomers. Those who went on their first European package holiday, enjoyed a higher standard of living than their parents and had greater expectations regarding the quality of life. The relaxation of credit in the 1970s, our increasing affluence, the advance of choice and consumerism and the exponential growth of credit in the 1990s have contributed to a society that relies in part on debt.

What is the answer?

Some look to government – but based on the past it is hard to see any significant solution coming from Parliament. The answer probably isn't new, but a combination of options. Will there be a return to selling the parental home and moving in with children? We have moved away from this in recent years, but this is commonplace, even in some European countries. Downsizing? Continuing to work part-time? Subject to the economy there are often jobs that are geared towards pensioners looking for additional income. Pensioners also come with advantages, such as experience. Maybe there will be an increase in equity release schemes.

But how will those fare who are paying so much more for their properties than was the case for today's pensioners? For many who are saddled with debt today, contemplating how retirement will look is probably too remote a scenario. Having to cope with increased energy, food and mortgage costs is about as much as many can contemplate.

We could dissect the state of our finances in more depth. There are many who write and analyse the state of the nation's finances on the Internet or the weekend newspapers. Your money counts to you and probably those close to you. The world's economy is in a mess. Some of those institutions that have been responsible for sub-prime loans, extending credit and unsecured loans have themselves mismanaged their finances. As a result they ask shareholders for money to bale them out of their predicament.

Your Money Counts gives an alternative approach to managing our finances. You will recognise many of the components and recommendations.

For those who believe in God and call Jesus Christ, 'Lord,' this book is based on what the Bible has to say. God's Word and prayer should be our first call, not our last resort.

However, if like I did, you find yourself at a point where nothing else has worked, and you feel like you are at a 'walls of Jericho' moment, take heart, God loves you and His Word never fails. We will outline simple practical steps you can pursue in order to make lasting changes to managing your own finances. But firstly I would like to introduce you to a guaranteed investment

three
A guaranteed investment

Now, if you do not call yourself a Christian but have got this far, well done – don't quit now. This chapter will say a little more about God and His Son, Jesus Christ. The rest of this book will say a lot more about money: how you can find financial freedom, not worry about money and manage money better, reduce your debts, save for your own future and the future of those you love and about being generous." You may have been to church for weddings and funerals and on other occasions when persuaded, but let me guess, somehow you don't feel God or religion is for you. Like many things in life, money is uncertain. We cannot be sure what is going to happen in the future. But Christians believe that there is an investment we can make that has a guaranteed return.

Let's look at the Bible

Bible simply means 'books.' It is the book that has been sold more than any other book – including James Bond and all of J K Rowling's books put together. It is also the oldest book on sale and it took longer to write than any other book. It is a book that is believed by many famous people, not just Cliff Richard!

The Bible comprises 66 different books. These were written over a period of 1500 years by 44 different authors whose occupations were as diverse as kings, peasants, philosophers, fisherman and scholars. It was written on three different continents – Asia, Africa and Europe – in three languages – Hebrew, Aramaic and Greek. The Bible ultimately has one author and editor – God himself. In the 60th verse of the 55th book we find that "all Scripture is God breathed" (2 Timothy 3:16).

The Bible has 1189 chapters and 31,173 verses. Like every good book the Bible tells you at the beginning what the book is about: it's God's story or

HIStory. He was there in the beginning. While every good book tells us how everything ends up, the last book only takes us so far; it isn't in fact the end. Just as this book believes that there is life after debt, so Christians believe that God promises eternal life after death for all those who believe in Jesus. Now, every good book has a turning point in the middle where the story turns and the mystery starts to unravel. So, let's visit the middle verse of the Bible and see if it passes the test. The middle verse (Psalm 118:8) says, "It is better to take refuge in the Lord than to trust in man."

You might ask me "Do you really believe all of this? How can you be sure?"

Yes, I do. As my story told I accepted Jesus as my Saviour when I was twelve. I have had more than 40 years to prove that God loves me and that He is real and I am 100 percent confident that when I die I am going to heaven.

If this book was given to you, then ask the giver to share with you the good news of Jesus. We will in this chapter outline the key message of the Bible. This is a message that defines what the book is about and is based on the truth of that middle verse.

Having established the nature and purpose of the Bible we will start to cross reference what we are saying to verses in the Bible, these references will be shown in brackets for easy reading. There are many different translations of the Bible. The letters following the Bible verses (e.g. TLB, NLT) tell you which translation has been used. Where no letters follow the verse then this is from the New International Version, the NIV.

God loves you and wants you to know Him

God created people in His own image, and He desires an intimate relationship with each of us. "For God so loved the world that He gave his only Son, that whoever believes in Him shall not perish but have eternal life" (John 3:16). We also read that "My (Jesus') purpose is to give life in all its fullness" (John 10:10, TLB).

We are separated from God

God is holy. This means God is perfect, and He does not have a relationship with anyone who is not perfect. "For all have sinned and fallen short of the glory of God" (Romans 3:23). Sin separates us from God. "Your sins have cut you off from God" (Isaiah 59:2).

This diagram illustrates our separation from God.

An enormous gap separates us from God. Individuals try without success to bridge this gap through their own efforts, such as living a good, moral life or doing good deeds.

God's only provision to bridge this gap: Jesus Christ

Jesus Christ died on the cross to pay the penalty for our sin and bridge the gap between us and God. Jesus said, "I am the way and the truth, and the life; no one comes to the Father (God) except through me" (John 14:6). "But God demonstrates his own love for us in this: While we were still sinners, Christ died for us" (Romans 5:8).

This diagram illustrates our union with God through Jesus Christ.

This relationship is a gift from God

As an act of faith you can also receive the free gift of a life in an eternal relationship with God. Free? Yes. "For it is by grace you have been saved, through faith – and this is not from yourselves, it is the gift of God – not by works, so that no-one can boast" (Ephesians 2:8-9).

We must all receive Jesus Christ individually

At the age of twelve I only had to turn away (repent from) my sins and ask Jesus Christ to come into my life and become my Saviour and Lord. And I did.

After more than forty years as a Christian, I can confirm beyond a shadow of doubt that a relationship with God can be yours through Jesus Christ. Nothing I know compares with the privilege of knowing Christ personally.

If you desire to know the Lord and are not certain whether you have this relationship, I encourage you to ask Christ to come into your life by saying this prayer:

Father God, I need you. I admit I have done wrong and I want to turn away from that life. I invite you, Jesus, to come into my life and make me the person You want me to be. Thank you for forgiving my sins and giving me the gift of eternal life.

You might fulfil each of the principles in this book in becoming a faithful stewards of money, but without a relationship with Christ your efforts will be in vain. If you asked Christ into your life, begin to attend a church that teaches the Bible so that you can learn and mature in your faith.

Ready? In the next sixteen chapters we will look more closely at God's economy. As you will soon discover the Bible has much help and counsel regarding how we handle our money, wealth and possessions. God's economy does not falter like the world's and if you are struggling with your finances then please read on. Again, because of what we believe about the Bible we regularly quote from the Bible and give references should you wish to look up these verses.

four
The
problem

Jonathan and Helen Thompson decided to end their marriage of 11 years. In anticipation of the divorce settlement, Jonathan began to review the family's financial position. As he sorted through the files, he came across an old faded invoice from the hotel where he and Helen had stayed on their honeymoon. Another receipt was for an instalment on their first car. He picked up still another invoice and remembered with fatherly pride how he had paid for a school trip to France for their second child. And then there was the deposit payment on their first home, the credit card receipts for their first child's cot, the family's annual zoo entrance subscription, and the payment to tour Buckingham Palace….

After several hours of sorting through such papers, Jonathan realised how much he and his wife had invested in their marriage. He paused, deep in thought for several minutes. Then he closed the file and called his wife on her mobile. After an awkward exchange he blurted out the reason for his call. Would she work with him to rebuild their marriage?

While a family crisis such as Jonathan and Helen's may be alien to some of us, the message of their family's payments is common. It is the story of our lives. It tells us about our values, our priorities, our memories, how much we save, what we spend, to whom we give. In fact, our bank and credit card statements tell us more about our priorities than anything else.

God is our Creator and the Bible is our Creator's handbook. It is the only book He wrote and it tells His story. There are 31,173 verses and within those we find 2,350 that give advice and instruction on how we should handle our money, wealth and possessions. Jesus tells 38 stories in the New Testament to illustrate something He wished to teach; the Bible refers to these stories as 'parables.' Of these, 16 relate to how we handle our money, wealth and possessions; 15% of Jesus' recorded words relate to the subject. Indeed Jesus said more about money and possessions than about almost any other subject. The Bible offers 500 verses on prayer while fewer than 500 discuss faith.

The Lord Jesus said a lot about money and possessions because He wants us to know His perspective on this critical area of our life. He deals with financial matters because *money does matter*. Actually there are so many that want to have a say in how we manage our finances, whether it is in offering to extend credit or helping us save or spend. In fact they shout so loud we can hardly hear ourselves think! But it is important that we have the first word and the last word on what we do with our money. Western economies revolve around the world's system of spending and buying. We should be prepared to challenge the view that we should live for today without too much of an eye on the future; debt is desirable, affordable and necessary; investing is impossible when household finances are under such pressure. Your financial views may include one or more of these positions. Television and media commentators periodically focus intensely on the latest financial crisis, whether it is a 'pensions' crisis' or 'credit crunch.'

Having been a business adviser for more than 25 years I have experienced a number of recessions. I have seen families torn apart by financial crises. Is the Bible relevant, and if so in what way?

The Bible sets out God's perspective on how we should handle our finances. You may find most of what you will read obvious, but this may not always be the case. Where you find something that you consider obvious and relevant to you, ask, "am I doing it?" When you read something you are not doing, then ask, "do I agree?" God's economy fundamentally differs from that of the world's. Why? Because God has an eternal perspective – not a "spend and have or experience today" perspective.

five
The answer –
the Bible is a blueprint for living

I was packing away my notebook and papers into my briefcase when my phone rang. It was 5:30 p.m. and I was getting ready to go home after a long day of reviewing papers, answering letters and client meetings. I was tired. Reluctantly, I answered the phone.

"Hello, Mark. This is Jonathan Thompson."

I felt a pang of embarrassment. I had neglected to return his earlier call. He sounded depressed, and I made a lame apology for not calling him back.

"Helen and I considered a divorce, but we decided to try to work it out," he said, his voice sounding strained.

Their financial problems were on the verge of destroying their marriage. He asked if we could meet to discuss their situation. We knew each other at church where we had both been youth group leaders. This was Jonathan's second marriage and I knew from talking with him after leaders' meetings that he was experiencing personal difficulties. Jonathan earned a living as a distribution manager at a local brewery company, Helen as a part-time nurse. I knew they had a mortgage and that they found it difficult to work out where their money went. They faced increasing household costs with their growing family and they knew that some time in the future they would have to help with higher education costs for their three children. Jonathan had just been told his mortgage payment was due to increase by £150 a month and he could see no way they could afford the higher payment. Neither of them could see how they could cope, in fact all they could see was doom and gloom and an impossible situation.

In addition, the Thompsons owed a substantial amount to retail stores, unsecured loans, credit cards and their bank. They had a sizable home mortgage. Because of their debts and their increasing daily expenses, the Thompsons shopped carefully. They had stopped shopping at the large local supermarket and had moved to one of the lower cost stores three miles away. Helen always compared the cost of household goods on the Internet and was always looking out for those two-for-one offers. Jonathan did most of the car repairs, and Helen avoided buying expensive clothes. But the family faced a critical problem. Helen and Jonathan did not have a clear guideline for handling money. They had never been able to budget their spending. They seldom decided not to buy what they wanted, and they had no plan to save or invest for the future.

I understood their predicament. When I was just married and training to be an accountant I too had little income. I had met Rhoda and she was looking after Philip. Rhoda took on a part-time evening job while I studied at home. We had no mortgage as we rented a flat, but we did have credit card debt and an overdraft. Even though I was training to be an accountant I still had not seen the need to compile a budget. Ted Kent, a visiting church speaker stayed at our home and shared with us what the Bible has to say about getting out of debt. That was the first time I saw that the Bible had something to say about our finances. I had put my trust in God and accepted Jesus as Saviour, so I knew much about what God had to say about how to live in other areas of my life. I had just missed the bit about finances! I resolved to study and then seek to help others see what the Bible has to say about finances. I had always been interested in delving deep into a subject, including creation, faith, prayer, the life of Jesus, the Jews and Arabs in the Bible (when I was a teenager I watched the Six Day War reported on the television and wanted to understand the roots of the ongoing Middle East conflict).

One day my church leader asked me to teach on biblical financial principles. I prepared as well I could, bringing together all I could find in the Bible on handling money, wealth and possessions. After I had spoken for an hour people bombarded me with questions and asked for help in areas they found difficult to understand – that was a learning curve for me as well as those who attended. Other churches asked me to speak, often when the church needed finance! Little did I know that over in America Howard Dayton and others were similarly being led to study the Bible in this area of stewardship. Howard developed his talks into a small group financial study which today is used in more than 60 countries.

This knowledge and insight from the Bible has helped millions of people like the Thompsons. We have found that many people either do not know or are not adopting these principles in their lives. Applying these principles is crucial for three reasons:

1. How we handle money affects our fellowship with the Lord

In Luke 16:11 we read, "Therefore if you have not been faithful in the use of unrighteous wealth, who will entrust the true riches to you?" (NASB). In this verse Jesus equates how we handle our money with the quality of our spiritual life. If we handle our money properly according to the principles of Scripture, our fellowship with Christ will grow stronger. However, if we manage money unfaithfully, our fellowship with Him will suffer.

Someone once told me that the Lord often allows a person to teach a subject because he or she needs to develop and mature in that area. That has certainly been true for me in the area of money. I have had the privilege of counselling hundreds of people and leading many Crown small groups, I thank God I was able to learn and apply these biblical financial principles from my early twenties. Others testify how they have changed their attitude to money and have experienced a meaningful improvement in their fellowship with the Lord.

2. Possessions compete with the Lord

Possessions are a primary competitor with Christ for lordship of our lives. Jesus tells us we must choose to serve only one of these two masters: "No-one can serve two masters. Either he will hate the one and love the other, or he will be devoted to the one and despise the other. You cannot serve both God and Money" (Matthew 6:24). It is impossible for us to serve money – even in a small way – and still serve the Lord.

When the Crusades were being fought during the 12th century, the crusaders employed mercenaries to fight on their behalf. Because it was a religious war, the crusaders insisted that the mercenaries be baptised before fighting. As they were being baptised, the mercenaries would hold their swords out of the water to symbolise the one thing in their life that Jesus Christ did not control. They had the freedom to use the swords in any way they wished.

Today many people handle their money in a similar fashion, though they may not be as obvious about it. They hold their wallet or purse "out of the water," in effect saying, *"God, You can be the Lord of my entire life except for my money. I am perfectly capable of handling that myself."*

3. Much of life revolves around the use of money

During your normal week, how much time do you spend earning money in your job, making decisions on how to spend money, thinking about where to save and invest money or praying about your giving? Fortunately, God has prepared us adequately for these tasks by giving us the Bible as His blueprint for handling money.

The answer

With the twenty-first century seeing so much financial upheaval people increasingly wonder where they can turn for help. There are two basic alternatives: the Bible and the answers people devise. The way most people handle money is in sharp contrast to God's financial principles. Isaiah 55:8 reads, "'For my thoughts are not your thoughts, neither are your ways my ways, declares the Lord" (NKJV). To help the reader recognise the differences between these two ways, a brief comparison appears at the end of each chapter under the heading "Contrast."

Learning to be content

When contentment is mentioned in the Bible, it more often than not refers to money. In Philippians 4:11–13 Paul writes,

---

I have learned to be content whatever the circumstances. I know what it is to be in need, and I know what it is to have plenty. I have learned the secret of being content in any and every situation, whether well fed or hungry, whether living in plenty or in want. I can do everything through him who gives me strength.

Philippians 4:11–13

Examine these verses carefully. We are not born with the instinct for contentment; rather it is learned.

My purpose for this book is to help you learn the biblical principles of handling money and possessions. The book will offer you practical ways to integrate these principles into your life. You don't have to be an accountant to implement these principles. A Christian knows the Bible is the Creator's handbook and Paul tells us in 2 Timothy 3:16 that "All Scripture is God-breathed and is useful for teaching, rebuking, correcting and training in righteousness, so that the man of God may be thoroughly equipped for every good work." As you discover these principles and put them into practice, you will draw closer to Christ, submit more fully to Him as Lord, learn to be content and set your financial house in order.

Contrast

Society says: God plays no role in handling money and my happiness is based on being able to afford my desired standard of living.

Scripture says: As you learn and follow the scriptural principles of how to handle money, you will draw close to Christ and learn to be content in every circumstance.

six
God's part –
the foundation

On a rainy November Saturday morning Jonathan and Helen Thompson arrived at my home to work through their financial problems in an attempt to save their marriage.

Jonathan and Helen were Christians, but they had never been exposed to the Bible's perspective on money and possessions. They appreciated their beautiful two-story brick house in Bristol, their two recently acquired cars and their other possessions. Both felt that they had worked hard for what they had and that they had earned the right to enjoy 'the good life'. However, after financial pressures threatened their standard of living, their lack of contentment surfaced in a major marital crisis. A serious lack of communication existed regarding their family finances. Jonathan and Helen each had their own opinions on how to spend the family income, and they had never been able to discuss the subject without ending up in an argument.

They were close to losing everything to their creditors. That, coupled with the possibility of divorce, had jarred them from their complacency. So when we sat down with Jonathan and Helen they were motivated to learn what the Bible says about money.

Scripture teaches there are two distinct parts to the handling of our money: (1) the part God plays and (2) the part we play. I believe most of

Everything in the heavens
and earth is yours, O Lord,
and this is your kingdom.
We adore you as being in
control of everything.
Riches and honour come
from you alone, and you
are the Ruler of all
mankind; your hand
controls power and might,
and it is at your discretion
that men are made great
and given strength.

King David
1 Chronicles 29:11–12, TLB

the confusion relating to the handling of money arises from the fact that these two parts are not clearly understood.

God's part is the foundation of contentment. In Scripture God calls Himself by more than 250 names. The name that best describes God's part in the area of money is *Master*. This is the most important chapter of the entire book because how we view God determines how we live. For example, after losing his children and all his possessions, Job was still able to worship God. He knew the Lord and the Lord's role as Master of those possessions. Similarly, Moses forsook the treasures of Egypt and chose to suffer mistreatment with the people of God. Both Job and Moses knew the Lord and accepted His role as Master.

Let's examine what the Bible has to say about God's part in three crucial areas: ownership, control and provision.

Ownership

The Bible clearly states that God is sole owner of everything. "The earth is the Lord's, and everything in it, the world, and all who live in it;" (Psalm 24:1). Scripture even reveals specific items God owns. Leviticus 25:23 identifies Him as owner of all the land: "the land must not be sold permanently, because the land is mine." Haggai 2:8 reveals that "the silver is mine and the gold is mine,' declares the Lord Almighty." And in Psalm 50:10, the Lord tells us "For every animal of the forest is mine, and the cattle on a thousand hills."

The Lord is the Creator of all things, and He has never transferred the ownership of His creation to people. In Colossians 1:17 we are told that "in Him all things hold together." At this very moment the Lord literally holds everything together by His power. Recognising God's ownership is critical in order to allow Jesus Christ to become the Lord of our money and possessions.

Ownership or Lordship?

If we are going to be genuine followers of Christ, we must transfer the ownership of our possessions to the Lord. "Any of you who does not give up everything he has cannot be my disciple" (Luke 14:33). In my experience and the experience of others I have found that the Lord will sometimes test us by asking if we are willing to relinquish a possession that is dear to us. Our church pastor's wife struggled with accepting that God owned her diamonds. We were holding a Crown study and looking at the passages of Scripture about God owning everything. As we were signing our Deed of Ownership (see page 40) she refused not; no way was she going to sign the Deed and accept that God owns her diamond jewellery. Then returning from the mid-course break she announced "that's it – I'm ready to sign." One week later God spoke to her and she readily gave away one piece of her jewellery.

Don't let this alarm you! God does not always take from us the things we value. Much more often he allows and takes pleasure in our enjoyment of these things. The point is that ultimately these things belong to the Lord.

Scripture's most vivid example of this is when the Lord told Abraham "take now your son, your only son Isaac, whom you love, …and offer him there as a burnt offering" (Genesis 22:2 NKJV). When Abraham obeyed, demonstrating his willingness to give up his dearest possession, God provided a substitute ram for the offering, and Isaac was not harmed.

When we acknowledge God's ownership, spending decisions becomes spiritual decisions. No longer do we ask, 'Lord, what do You want me to do with *my* money?' The question is restated as 'Lord, what do You want me to do with Your money?' When we have this perspective, spending and saving decisions are equally as spiritual as giving decisions.

The first step toward contentment

To learn to be content, you must recognise God as the owner of all your possessions. If you believe you own even a single possession, then the circumstances affecting that possession will be reflected in your *attitude*. If something favourable happens to that possession, then you will be happy. But if something bad occurs, you will be discontented.

When we were training with Crown in Atlanta we were lent an Old Town Lincoln car by Bill and Ruth Swaim, who had decided they wanted to help us. You often see these cars in films; they are the original big

American gas guzzlers. The car had clocked 150,000 miles and was Bill's pride and joy. In December as we returned from watching Howard record a Crown radio programme we were involved in a head-on accident with the driver of a white van. He decided to overtake without checking to see if the road was clear. We were forcefully shunted into a ditch, but miraculously saved from serious injury. The car was solid and its armour-like chassis protected us as we rolled over. While we survived, the car did not. How did Bill react when his trusty car was reduced to a wreck? Bill's first reaction, as he told us later, was that of 'disappointment,' the car held a lot of memories for him and his family. However, the Lincoln was his spare car, so imagine how we felt the next day when he gave us the keys to his own car – again another Old Town but more up to date. With a smile he gave us the keys and told us that God was teaching us all 'something about His ownership.' Similarly, when John Wesley learned that his home had been destroyed by fire, he exclaimed, "The Lord's house burned. One less responsibility for me!"

Yet it is not easy to maintain this perspective consistently. It is far too easy to think that the possessions we have and the money we earn are entirely the result of our skills and achievements. We find it difficult not to believe we have earned the right to their ownership. *I am the master of my fate*, the humanist says. *I alone own my possessions.* Obviously, this view of ownership is the prevailing one in our culture.

Giving up ownership is not easy, nor is it a once-and-for-all transaction. We constantly need to be reminded that God owns all our possessions.

Control

The second responsibility God has retained is ultimate control of every event that occurs upon the earth. Examine several of the names of God in Scripture: Master, Almighty, Creator, Shepherd, Lord of lords and King of kings. It's obvious who is in charge:

We adore you as being in control of everything. Riches and honour come from you alone, and you are the Ruler of all mankind; your hand controls power and might, and it is at your discretion that men are made great and given strength.

1 Chronicles 29:11–12, TLB

Psalm 135:6 reads, "the Lord does whatever pleases him, in the heavens and on the earth." And in *Daniel 4:34–35* King Nebuchadnezzar "honoured and glorified him who lives for ever....He does as he pleases with the powers of heaven and the peoples of the earth. No-one can hold back his hand or say to him: What have you done?"

The Lord is in ultimate control of even difficult circumstances. "I am the Lord, and there is no other. I form the light and create darkness, I bring prosperity and create disaster; I, the Lord, do all these things" (Isaiah 45:6–7). It is important for the child of God to realise that his heavenly Father orchestrates even seemingly devastating circumstances for ultimate good in the lives of the godly. "And we know that God causes everything to work together for the good of those who love God and are called according to his purpose for them" (Romans 8:28 NLT).

Howard tells me that one of the most traumatic times he and Bev had in their marriage was when they were in the process of adopting their second son, Andrew. They received Andrew when he was four days old. He was an extraordinarily beautiful baby. When he was about three months old they noticed that he appeared to have physical problems. Howard and Bev went through two months of a roller-coaster experience with physicians unable to agree on a diagnosis.

Finally, they learned that his natural mother had used powerful drugs before and during the pregnancy, and Andrew had been born with only the stem of his brain. In their pain and deep hurt they repeatedly returned to the foundational fact that their heavenly Father loved Andrew even more than they did and that God wanted to entrust him into their care for a season. They became close friends with Andrew's natural grandparents, and their family learned compassion for the disadvantaged. They saw the Lord provide Andrew with the very best care, and they experienced many blessings in the midst of that emotional time.

The Lord allows difficult circumstances for three reasons:

1. To accomplish His intentions

This is illustrated in the life of Joseph who, as a teenager, was sold into slavery by his jealous brothers. Years later Joseph told his brothers "but don't be upset, and don't be angry with yourselves for selling me to this place. It was God who sent me here ahead of you to preserve your lives.... So it *was God who sent me here, not you*" (Genesis 45:5 and 8, emphasis added, NLT).

2. To develop our character

Godly character, something that is precious in the sight of the Lord, is often developed in the midst of trying times. Romans 5:3–4 reads "and not only *that*, but we also glory in tribulations, knowing that tribulation produces perseverance; and perseverance, character; and character, hope" (NKJV). Writing on this theme, A.W. Tozer, an American pastor and author said, "God can't use a person to the maximum, until he or she has been hurt deeply." I believe this is true. I've learned lessons of trusting the Lord and drawing close to Him that I never would have learned apart from difficult times.

3. To discipline His children

When we are disobedient, we can expect our loving Lord to administer discipline to encourage us to abandon our sin. This often comes through difficult circumstances.

Because the Lord disciplines those he loves…God disciplines us for our good, that we may share in his holiness. No discipline seems pleasant at the time, but painful. Later on, however, it produces a harvest of righteousness and peace for those who have been trained by it.
Hebrews 12:6,10–11

The Lord has control over every circumstance you will ever face. You can be content in knowing that your loving heavenly Father intends to use each situation ultimately for a good purpose.

Provision

The third element of God's part is that He has promised to provide for our needs. "But seek first the kingdom of God and His righteousness, and all these things shall be added to you" (Matthew 6:33, NKJV). In Genesis 22:14, God is spoken of as "Jehovah-jireh," which means "the Lord will provide." He takes care of His people, and He does not need a prosperous economy to provide for them. Each day He gave manna to the children of Israel during their 40 years of wandering in the wilderness. Jesus fed more than 5,000 with only five loaves and two fish.

God is both predictable and unpredictable. He is absolutely predictable in His faithfulness to provide for our needs. What we cannot predict is how the Lord will provide. He uses various and sometimes surprising means of meeting our needs. He may increase our income, provide a gift or stretch our limited resources through money-saving purchases; 'God is so good' is a phrase that Rhoda and I use frequently. He has provided for us so often and in so many unexpected ways.

When we were starting to work for Crown I submitted my first order to them for the Crown study guides. It was nine o'clock in the morning and as I looked at the screen I realised that I had made a costing error of £500. "And you are an accountant!," I thought to myself. We were going to import the studies which included what I considered to be a high delivery charge from the US. At 11 o'clock a friend came round to give me a cheque and to tell me how he felt prompted to make the gift. As this was the first cheque we had received I thanked him as I placed it on my desk. We talked for a further hour before I felt I should open the folded cheque, which I saw was for £500. Now I know this reads like a neat story, but we all have the same loving heavenly Father regardless of gender, colour, social status or whichever group you may regard yourself as a member. He is our provider. Regardless of how He chooses to provide for our needs, He is utterly reliable.

The first letter to Timothy 6:8 tells us that our needs are food and covering. In other words, there is a difference between needs and wants. A need is a basic necessity of life – food, clothing or shelter. A want is anything more than a need. A steak dinner, a new car and the latest technology are all wants.

It is, however, a little more complex. Education and health care, for example, are also fundamental human needs. In a modern society the way we understand needs will change. For example, many people in Britain would say they need a car, especially in rural areas. A car may not be a true need but it might be an acceptable need. However, changing the car each year for the sake of change or choosing one for appearances rather than functionality or a car with a bad environmental record or simply for the gadgets in a newer model could not be described as a need.

God's part in helping us reach contentment is that He has obligated Himself to provide our needs, but not our wants. He tells us to be content when our needs are met, "if we have food and clothing, we will be content with that" (1 Timothy 6:8).

Let me illustrate God's provision with a story.

As World War II was drawing to a close, the Allied armies gathered up many hungry orphans. They were placed in camps where they were well-fed. Despite excellent care, they slept poorly. They seemed nervous and afraid. Finally, a psychologist came up with a solution. Each child was given a piece of bread to hold after he was put to bed. If he was hungry, more food was provided, but when he was finished, this particular piece of bread was just to be held – not eaten. The piece of bread produced wonderful results. The children went to bed, instinctively knowing they would have food to eat the next day. That guarantee gave the children a restful and contented sleep.[2]

Similarly, the Lord has given us His guarantee – our 'piece of bread.' As we cling to His promises of provision, we can relax and be content. "And my God will meet all your needs according to his glorious riches in Christ Jesus" (Philippians 4:19). So even if you are in the middle of an extreme financial problem, you can be content because the Lord has promised to feed, clothe and shelter you.

I am convinced that the Lord will provide – at just the right time – the resources necessary for us to fulfil the purpose and calling He has for each of us. This is illustrated in 2 Samuel 12:7–8 when He spoke to David through Nathan the prophet: "You are the man! This is what the Lord, the God of Israel, says: 'I anointed you king over Israel, and I delivered you from the hand of Saul. I gave your master's house to you, and your master's wives into your arms. I gave you the house of Israel and Judah. And if all this had been too little, I would have given you even more.'"

From the life of David we see that God did not provide all the necessary resources for him to be king all at once. They came at the appropriate time, as David needed them. Occasionally, the Lord has withheld resources from Crown Financial Ministries. Howard tells me how sometimes he was confused when this occurred. He subsequently realised that if Crown had received the money too early, they would not have spent it the way that God intended.

Getting to know God

The basic reason we fail to recognise God's part is that we do not understand who God is. We often have no genuine awe for the Lord "Who stretched out the heavens and laid the foundations of the earth" (Isaiah

51:13). We tend to shrink God down and fit Him into a mould with human abilities and limitations. However, we can expand our vision to capture the true perspective of God by studying what the Bible tells us about Him. The following is just a sample:

Lord of the universe

The Lord's power is incomprehensible to humans. For example, astronomers estimate more than 100 billion galaxies exist in the universe, each containing billions of stars. The distance from one end of a galaxy to the other is often measured in thousands of light years. Our solar system is located in the Milky Way galaxy, which stretches 100 thousand light years across – that's pretty big! In fact calculations show that our solar system, relative to a 10p coin, is an area the size of North America. Yet God, the creator of the heavens and earth knows your name! The universe's enormity is beyond our comprehension. Isaiah 40:26 reads "lift your eyes and look to the heavens: Who created all these? He who brings out the starry host one by one, and calls them each by name. Because of his great power and mighty strength, not one of them is missing."

Lord of the nations

Examine the Lord's role and position relative to nations and people. Isaiah 40:21–24 tells us "have you not known? Have you not heard...? He who sits above the circle of the earth, and its inhabitants are like grasshoppers.... He brings the princes to nothing; He makes the judges of the earth useless. Scarcely shall they be planted, scarcely shall they be sown, scarcely shall their stock take root in the earth, when He will also blow on them, and they will wither" (NKJV).

And from Isaiah 40:15, 17 we read "behold, the nations *are* as a drop in a bucket, and are counted as the small dust on the scales...all nations before Him *are* as nothing, and they are counted by Him less than nothing and worthless" (NKJV).

Lord of the individual

God is not an aloof, disinterested 'force.' Rather, He is intimately involved with each of us as individuals. Psalm 139:3–4, 16 reveals "you discern my going out and my lying down; you are familiar with all my ways. Before a word is on my tongue you know it completely, O Lord....All the days ordained for me were written in your book before one of them came to be."

The Lord is so involved in our lives that He reassures us "even the very hairs of your head are all numbered" (Matthew 10:30). Our heavenly Father is the One who knows us best and loves us the most.

God hung the stars in space, fashioned the earth's towering mountains and mighty oceans, and determined the destiny of nations. Jeremiah observed correctly "nothing is too hard for you" (Jeremiah 32:17). Yet God knows when a sparrow falls to the ground. He is the Lord of the infinite and the infinitesimal.

In summary, let's review what God's part is. He is the owner, He is in control of every circumstance and He has promised to meet our needs. In other words, God who created the world and holds it together is able to perform His responsibilities and keep His promises. However, God's part is only half of the equation. It is the most important part, but it is only half. In the next chapter we will begin to examine the other half – our part.

Contrast

Society says: What I possess I alone own and I alone control my destiny.

Scripture says: What I possess God owns. He is the sovereign, living God who controls all events.

At the end of most chapters, after the CONTRAST between society and Scripture, there will be a COMMITMENT section that will give you the opportunity to practice the biblical principle we have just covered. I challenge and encourage you to 'do' the COMMITMENT sections because they will help make the principles a part of your life.

Commitment

In the Crown Financial Ministries small group study we go through an exercise of transferring the ownership of our possessions to the Lord. We use a deed to do this because a deed is often used to transfer the ownership of property. When participants in the Crown study complete and sign the deed, they are acknowledging that God is owner of their assets. The exercise is important because we all occasionally forget that God owns everything. We act as if we own it all. By signing the deed, a person establishes a specific time when God's ownership and your stewardship is acknowledged. Thus, a person can refer to the document repeatedly and recall that God owns everything.

The following will help you complete the deed:

1. Insert today's date
2. Sign your name. You are the one declaring God's ownership
3. Give prayerful consideration to the possessions you wish to acknowledge God owns. Then list those items
4. On the lower right-hand corner there is a space for the signature of witnesses. These friends can help hold you accountable for recognising God as owner of your possessions

DEED OF OWNERSHIP

This Deed of Ownership is made the _____ day of _____

From: _____

To: The Lord

On this day I/we acknowledge God's ownership and my/our stewardship responsibility of the following:

    ITEMS:

Stewards of the possessions listed above:

(Optional) witnesses who hold me/us accountable in the recognition of the Lord's ownership:

_____

_____

_____

_____

This instrument is not a binding legal document and cannot be used to transfer property.

seven
Our part – good and faithful

After he and Helen finished signing the deed, Jonathan slid it across the desk. "I feel a lot of relief," he said. "But I also feel like I'm supposed to do something." Jonathan was right. We cannot just sit back, do nothing and wait for God to perform. We have a responsibility. But, like Jonathan, we may not know exactly what our part is.

God, the Master, is the owner of everything, the controller of all events and our provider. Our responsibility is to be a steward. The word for steward can be translated into two different words: *manager* and *supervisor*. In Scripture the position of a steward is one of great responsibility. He or she is the supreme authority under the master and has full responsibility for all the master's possessions and household affairs.

> *Well done, good and faithful servant! You have been faithful with a few things; I will put you in charge of many things. Come and share your master's happiness!*
>
> **Matthew 25:21**

As we examine Scripture we see that God, as Master, has given us the authority to be stewards. "You (God) made him (people) ruler over the works of your hands; you put everything under his feet" (Psalm 8:6).

Our only responsibility is to be faithful. "Moreover it is required in stewards that one be found faithful" (1 Corinthians 4:2, NKJV). Before we

Contentment is the by-product of the faithful discharge of our duties.

can be faithful, we must know what we are required to do. Just as the purchaser of a car studies the manufacturer's manual to learn how to properly operate the car, we need to study our owner's handbook, the Bible, to find out how He wants us to handle His possessions. Several elements of faithfulness are important to understand.

1. Faithful with all our resources

We are charged to be faithful in handling 100 percent of our income, not just 10 percent. Unfortunately, many churches have concentrated only on teaching how to handle 10 percent of our income – the area of giving. Although this area is crucial, we have allowed Christians to learn how to handle the other 90 percent from the world's perspective, not from our Lord's perspective. Because they do not know how to handle money biblically, many Christians have wrong attitudes about possessions and make incorrect financial decisions that lead to painful consequences. Hosea 4:6 reads "my people are destroyed from lack of knowledge" Ignorance of or disobedience to scriptural financial principles frequently causes money problems.

2. Faithful regardless of how much we have

The issue in Scripture is how to handle faithfully all God has entrusted to us. The faithful steward is responsible for what he or she has, whether it is much or little. The parable of the talents illustrates this. "It will be like a man going on a journey, who called his servants and entrusted his property to them. To one he gave five talents of money, to another two talents, and to another one talent, each according to his ability" (Matthew 25:14–15). When the master returned, he held each slave accountable for managing his possessions faithfully. The master commended the faithful slave who received the five talents: "Well done, good and faithful servant! You have been faithful with a few things; I will put you in charge of many things. Come and share your master's happiness!" (Matthew 25:21). Interestingly, the slave who had been given two talents received a reward equal to that given to the slave who had been given the five talents (see Matthew 25:23). We are required to be faithful whether we are given much or little. As someone once said "it's not what I would do if one million pounds were my lot; it's what I am doing with the ten pounds I've got." Wealth is not equally distributed. Around half the world's population lives on less than

£1 a day, while the purchasing power of that money is much less than £5. So, if you have £5 to spend on whatever you choose you probably rank as one of the wealthiest people in the world!

3. Faithfulness in little things

Luke 16:10 reads "he who is faithful in a very little thing is faithful also in much; and he who is unrighteous in a very little thing is unrighteous also in much" (NASB). How do you know if a young adult is going to take good care of his first car? Observe how he cared for his bicycle. How do you know if a salesperson will do a competent job of serving a large client? Observe how he or she served a small client. If we have the character to be faithful with small things, the Lord knows He can trust us with greater responsibilities.

"Small things are small things," Hudson Taylor, the missionary statesman, said "but faithfulness with a small thing is a big thing."

4. Faithfulness with another's possessions

Faithfulness with another's possessions will, in some measure, determine the amount with which you are entrusted. "And if you have not been trustworthy with someone else's property, who will give you property of your own?" (Luke 16:12). This is a principle that is often overlooked. Are you faithful with another's possessions? Are you careless with your employer's office supplies? Do you waste electricity when you are staying in a hotel room? When someone allows you to use something, are you careful to return it in good condition? I am certain some people have not been given more because they have been unfaithful with the possessions of others.

5. Faithfulness builds character

God uses money to refine our character. In 1918 David McConaughy wrote a book, *Money, the Acid Test*. In it he said:

Money, most common of temporal things, involves uncommon and eternal consequences. Even though it may be done quite unconsciously, money moulds people – in the process of getting it, of saving it, of using it, of giving it, of accounting for it. Depending upon how it is handled, it proves a blessing or a curse to its possessor; either the person becomes master of the money, or the money becomes master of the person. Our Lord takes money, the thing that, essential though it is to our common life, sometimes seems so sordid, and he makes it a touchstone to test the lives of people and an instrument for moulding them into the likeness of himself.[3]

Clearly, if we are handling our possessions as faithful stewards, our character is being built. If we are unfaithful, our character is being compromised and harmed. For most of us there are three aspects of our lives which we consider every day: health, relationships and finances. Jesus Christ said more about money than any other single thing because money is of first importance when it comes to a person's real nature. How we handle money is an exact index to our true character. Throughout Scripture we find an intimate correlation between the development of a person's character and how he or she handles money."

6. Faithfulness leads to contentment

Once we know God's part and our part and faithfully do our part, we can be content. In Philippians we discover that Paul has learned to be content because he knew that God would supply all his needs (Philippians 4:19), and he had been faithful. "Whatever you have learned or received or heard from me, or seen in me – put it into practice" (Philippians 4:9).

As we apply the principles of God's economy, we *will* begin to get out of debt, spend more wisely, start saving for our future goals and give even more to the work of Christ. The Bible offers real solutions to today's financial problems. Each of the following chapters deals with one of the specific areas necessary to equip us to become faithful stewards.

At the beginning of most of the remaining chapters we will complete the section of the wheel of faithfulness to help clarify the responsibilities of a faithful steward.

Contrast

Society says: You earned your money, now spend it any way you choose and you'll be happy.

Scripture says: You can only be content if you have been a faithful steward handling money from the Lord's perspective.

eight
Debt –
act your own wage

The most immediate financial problem facing Jonathan and Helen was pressure from their creditors. And creditors they had! They had two loans from a bank, overdue statements from three department stores and outstanding balances on an assortment of credit cards. And then there was the mortgage.

The Thompson's indebtedness started soon after they had married

> *Out of debt, out*
> *of danger*
>
> **Proverb**

when they applied for their first loan. Helen, who grew up in an averagely wealthy family, said "our friends had new cars, and we felt deprived. We had to have a new car too." Later, when they moved to Bristol, they bought a house on the outskirts of the city, borrowing for the deposit payment. The debts continued to mount up. "Finally," Helen said, "the man from the bank told us he was going to repossess our house."

"Most of our debts were accumulated so slowly over the years," Jonathan said "that we didn't realise what was happening until it was too late."

Each year millions of people find themselves in the Thompsons' predicament. A credit expert says the major reason is "damage to the borrower's ability to pay." People take out loans on the assumption they will have a steady flow of income; then the unexpected happens. Someone gets sick. A new baby is on the way. An employer goes out of business.

Debt increasing

Government, business and personal debt is exploding in our nation. If you converted the total debt into £5 notes, placed them end to end, they would extend more than 17 million miles or the equivalent of about 150 return journeys to the moon. At over two trillion pounds national and personal debt is more than £30,000 for *every* UK resident. The average interest payment per household is approaching £4,000 per annum. The economy is riding on a growing mountain of debt.

With students trained to be dependent on debt, and with housing, energy and basic living costs at such a high proportion of most people's income, it is not surprising there are many who cannot manage financially Paying the mortgage is most people's main financial priority, settling unsecured monthly debt repayments is sometimes an account for which little or no funds exist. There are now more credit cards in circulation today than there are people living in this country. As the number of cars on the road increases so do the number of accidents; as the amount of unsecured debt increases there will be more casualties.

In a recent year there were more than 100,000 individual insolvencies, including more than 40,000 Individual Voluntary Arrangements (IVAs). The average age of a bankrupt is someone in their forties. It is estimated that the average household has to work for more than 75 days to pay the mortgage interest. More sobering is the fact that many divorces cite tensions concerning finance as a factor in the breakdown of their relationship. For many, the more accurate marriage vow would have been 'till debt do us part.' Such financial tension exists largely because consumers believe the 'gospel of buy it because you deserve it' or, 'buy now and pay later with easy monthly payments.' We all know that nothing about those monthly payments is easy.

In an endeavour to win business some advertise, 'buy now, no repayments for two (or more) years! There are a myriad of schemes designed to encourage you to buy 'stuff' that does not have to be paid for today. I received a letter from my car manufacturer advising that the warranty was about to expire. For £900 I could renew my warranty; I was of course encouraged to pay this monthly. I visited the local main dealer and was told that their cost was only £550, and I could pay this monthly over three years. At which point Simon, my youngest son, pointed out that if I paid for the warranty in this manner in the future I would end up making three years' payments each month – two of which would be for a lapsed warranty.

While in the US we found ourselves flicking through the 75 or so TV channels, each one with endless intermissions for the advertisements. It seemed that more than 50 percent of those advertisements involved 'easy payments.' The actual cost of the item received no mention, all that mattered was the 'easy' cost per month.

There is nothing easy about these payments. There are those who say we always follow the Americans, and those who say that in this regard we already have. Proverbs 22:7 informs us that the borrower is slave to the lender. Jesus came to set us free so that we need not be bondage – how

important is it to free yourself from debt so that you can celebrate being debt free? How important is it to take action so that you can freely plan your finances the way that God intends?

> Just as the rich rule the poor, so the borrower is servant to the lender.
>
> **King Solomon,**
> **Tenth century, B.C.**

What is debt?

Lenders and advertisers use attractive definitions of debt that mask its harsh reality. Roget's Thesaurus lists the following synonyms for debt: bankrupt, indebted, insolvent, obliged. Do you feel uncomfortable as you read this list? I have yet to see one advertisement that promises the good life of 'buy now and pay later' balanced with these words that describe the reality of debt. Are you beginning to have the feeling that the gospel of 'buy it because you deserve it' might not be preaching the whole truth of the abundant life as a member of the 'debt set?'

The Oxford dictionary defines debt as 'a sum of money owed.' Debt includes money owed to credit-card companies, bank loans, money borrowed from relatives, consumer loans, consolidation loans and the home mortgage. Bills that become due in the month, such as any monthly account, e.g. window cleaning, are not considered debt provided they are paid on time. However, some utility bills may have an outstanding balance that is not covered by the ongoing monthly direct debits and, to that extent, there may be debt rolled up into these accounts. This occurs when energy costs increase and there is no prompt action to increase the utility payments. One course of action here is to contact the utility company and revise payments for it is better to act sooner than later. Where if utility bills are estimated, read your meter and update your supplier to ensure you are not taken unaware by an actual account that is higher than the estimate.

What does debt really cost?

We need to recognise the true cost of debt. Two common types of debt are the credit card and the home mortgage.

Credit card debt

Please study the chart on page 49.

1. Assume you have £5,560 in credit card debt at an interest rate of 18 percent. This would cost about £1,000 in interest annually. Over 40 years the total interest payable would be £40,000.
2. Look at line 2. As an alternative to paying interest, what would be the effect of saving £83.33 a month (£1,000 a year)? Over 40 years you would receive a return of £119,405, a return approaching 300 percent in addition to the £40,000 of your own capital, making a total investment of £159,405.
3. Line 3 looks at what the lender earns at 18 percent. The lender's gross earnings from the interest at £83.33 interest a month amount to a staggering £4,497,902, a return of 11,245 percent.

You can see what lenders have known for a long time – compounding interest has an incredible impact. It can work for you, or it can work against you. Is there any wonder credit card companies are eager for you to become one of their borrowers?

1. Amount of interest you would pay annually:				
Year 1	Year 10	Year 20	Year 30	Year 40
£1,000	£10,000	£20,000	£30,000	£40,000
2. What interest you earn with a £1,000 annual investment at 6 percent:				
Year 1	Year 10	Year 20	Year 30	Year 40
£30	£3,576	£17,888	£51,430	£119,405
3. What the lender earns from your £1,000 annual payment at 18 percent:				
Year 1	Year 10	Year 20	Year 30	Year 40
£90	£15,638	£139,824	£832,133	£4,497,902

Home mortgage

A 25-year home mortgage, at an APR of 7 percent, will require you to pay more than twice the amount originally borrowed.

Original mortgage amount	£120,000
Monthly mortgage payment at 7 percent interest	£831.74
Months paid	x 300
Total payment	£249,524
Total interest paid	£129,524

Debt also extracts a physical toll. It often increases stress, which contributes to mental, physical and emotional fatigue. It can stifle creativity and harm relationships. Many people raise their standard of living through debt, only to discover that the burden of debt controls their lifestyles. The car sticker that reads, "I owe, I owe, it's off to work I go," is an unfortunate reality for too many people.

What does scripture say about debt?

Scripture's perspective on debt is clear. Read the first portion of Romans 13:8 carefully from several different Bible translations: "Let no debt remain outstanding" (NIV). "Owe nothing to anyone" (NLT). "Keep out of debt and owe no man anything" (AMP).

In Proverbs 22:7 we are reminded why our Lord speaks so directly about debt: "Just as the rich rule the poor, so the borrower is servant to the lender" (NLT). When we are in debt, we are in a position of servitude to the lender. Indeed, the deeper we are in debt, the more of a servant we become. We do not have the full freedom or discretion to decide where to spend our income because we have legally obligated ourselves to meet these debts.

In 1 Corinthians 7:23 Paul writes "you were bought at a price; do not become slaves of men." Our Father made the ultimate sacrifice by giving His Son, the Lord Jesus Christ, to die for us. He now wants His children free to serve Him in whatever way He chooses.

Debt considered a curse

In the Old Testament one of the rewards for obedience was being out of debt. "If you fully obey the Lord your God and carefully follow all his commands that I give you today, the Lord your God will set you high above all the nations on earth. All these blessings will come upon you and accompany you…if you obey the Lord your God…if you obey the Lord your God…you will lend to many nations *but will borrow from none*" (Deuteronomy 28:1–2, 12, emphasis added).

Conversely, indebtedness was one of the curses inflicted for disobedience. "However, if you do not obey the Lord your God and do not carefully follow all his commands and decrees I am giving you today, all these curses will come upon you and overtake you.…The alien who lives among you will rise above you higher and higher, but you will sink lower and lower. *He will lend to you*, but you will not lend to him. He will be the head, but you will be the tail" (Deuteronomy 28:15, 43–44, emphasis added).

Debts can be cancelled and forgiven

Deuteronomy tells us that God's provision and a faithful, obedient people should mean that there are no poor in the land (Deuteronomy 15:4-5). But the same passage recognises that there will always be poor in the land (verse 11) and there are two implications. The first is that the people are instructed to lend freely to their neighbour (Deuteronomy 15:8) and this generosity in allowing others to borrow is a source of God's blessing. Secondly, every seven years all debts were to be cancelled (Deuteronomy 15:1-3) and that it was a selfish thought not to lend just before the cancellation of debts (verse 8). What can we learn? However trapped in debt we may be there is always hope. In our modern context this text does not permit people to borrow with no intent to repay. Nor, in principle, does it permit creditors to pursue repayments from those who cannot repay.

Debt presumes upon tomorrow

When we get into debt, we assume that we will earn enough or will have sufficient resources to pay the debt. We plan for our job to continue or our business or investments to be profitable. Scripture cautions us against presumption: "Now listen, you who say, 'Today or tomorrow we will go to this or that city, spend a year there, carry on business and make money.' Why, you do not even know what *will happen* tomorrow. What is your life? You are a mist that appears for a little while and then vanishes. Instead, you *ought* to say, 'If it is the Lord's will, we will live and do this or that'" (James 4:13–15).

Debt may deny God an opportunity to work

Financial author Ron Blue tells of a young man who wanted to go to Bible school to become a missionary. The young man had no money and thought the only way he could afford Bible school was to secure a student loan. However, this would have encumbered him with thousands of dollars of debt by the time he graduated. This would have been an impossible situation. He could not pay back his loan on a missionary's salary.

After a great deal of prayer, he decided to enrol without the help of a student loan and to trust the Lord to meet his needs. He graduated without borrowing anything and grew in his appreciation for how the sovereign, living God could creatively provide for his needs. This was the most valuable lesson learned in Bible School. It prepared him for the mission field where he repeatedly depended on the Lord to meet his needs. Borrowing may deny God an opportunity to demonstrate His reality.

When can we owe money?

Scripture is silent on the subject of when we can owe money. In my opinion it is possible to owe money for a home mortgage or for your business or, not withstanding the above story, vocational training. This 'possible debt' is permissible, we believe, only if the following four criteria are met:

1. The item purchased is an asset with the potential to appreciate or to produce an income
2. The value of the item equals or exceeds the amount owed against it
3. The debt is not so large that repayment puts undue strain on the budget
4. The debt does not cause anxiety (Isaiah 32:17)

Let me give you an example of how a home mortgage might qualify. Historically, the home has usually been an appreciating asset; therefore, it meets the first criterion. Second, if you invest a reasonable deposit, you could expect to sell the home for at least enough to repay the mortgage, and this meets the second requirement. Third, the monthly mortgage repayment should not strain your budget. If you meet all the criteria and assume some 'possible debt,' I hope you will immediately establish a goal to repay as quickly as practical. We cannot be certain that the housing market will appreciate or even maintain current values. Moreover, the loss of a job can interrupt your income. Therefore, I urge you to consider prayerfully paying off all debt.

Student debt?

Student debt poses a specific problem and is one that students must address, with or without parental assistance. For most, student debt is almost inevitable for those wishing to obtain a degree. In fact student debt is a particular type of debt. You will never secure another loan at such a low rate of interest nor one for which the repayments are directly linked to earnings. That said, it is still a burden of debt on people at the start of their adult lives. There is the danger that it creates in young people a culture of debt.

When Simon was planning to go to university he decided to go to a local university and live at home. We paid for his food and made no charge for rent. During the first two years he worked at a local petrol station and used the income to cover his personal costs. He tithed and saved 20% of his income. During his placement year he paid rent. He also earned some part-time income from designing and photography so that by the end of university he had saved £10,000 and had no student debt. With student debt at the time averaging £13,000, that seemed to be a positive £23,000 variance.

Now not for a moment am I suggesting everyone can do this. Not every family can support a student at home for a range of reasons. Not every student is able to work, while for many going away from home is part of the university experience. What is important is that students take a mature attitude to student debt, that they plan and live to a realistic budget and where possible work to minimise their debts. Once leaving higher education the repayment of student debt should be a priority over seeking an ever higher standard of living. There are over three million people who owe student debt.

nine
Getting out of debt – Debt Free Day

We have so much personal debt in our nation that the average person has been described as someone driving on a debt-financed road, in a bank-financed car, powered by credit card-financed fuel, going to purchase furniture on an instalment plan to put in his mortgage-financed home!

"I hope I never pick up another one," Jonathan said.

"I just didn't know," Helen recalled. "I had no experience."

What were they talking about? Poisonous reptiles? Radioactive material? Hard drugs?

No. Credit cards. The Thompsons had run up thousands of pounds of debt on credit cards and were paying a high rate of interest for that 'privilege.' This is a common predicament. The easy availability of credit has spawned phenomenal growth in the number of cards held by customers. The average consumer carries more than three cards in his wallet.

At the end of the initial meeting with the Thompsons, Jonathan asked for my scissors. He wanted to perform some 'plastic surgery.' As a symbol of their vow to get out of debt, he cut their credit cards to ribbons. If they follow through in their commitment, they will be in the minority. Less than 50 percent of those who take the initial step actually follow through on their commitment and become debt-free.

How to get out of debt

Because of your particular circumstances, your path for getting out of debt will be unique to you. The following 10 steps are a guide for your journey. The steps are simple, but following them requires hard work. The goal is Debt Free Day – debtless day, the day when you become absolutely free of debt.

1. Pray

In 2 Kings 4:1–7 a widow was threatened with losing her children to her creditor and she appealed to Elisha for help. Elisha instructed the widow to borrow many empty jars from her neighbours. The Lord supernaturally multiplied her only possession, a small quantity of oil, and as a result all the jars were filled. She sold the oil and paid her debts to free her children. The same God who provided supernaturally for the widow is interested in you becoming free of debt as well.

The first step is the most important. Pray. Ask for the Lord's help and guidance in your journey toward Debt Free Day. He might act immediately, as in the case of the widow, or slowly over time. In either case, prayer is essential.

I have observed a trend. As people begin to eliminate debt and accelerate debt repayment, the Lord blesses their faithfulness. Even if you can afford only a small monthly prepayment to reduce your debt, please do it. The Lord can multiply your efforts.

2. Establish a written budget

In my experience, few people in debt have been using a written budget. They may have had one, neatly filed away in a drawer, but they have not been using it. A written budget helps you plan ahead and analyse your spending patterns to see where you can minimise outgoings. It is an effective bridle on impulse spending.

3. List your assets – sell what you are not using

List every possession you own: your home, car, furniture, etc. Evaluate the complete list to determine whether you should sell any assets. As we began to consider items the Thompsons might sell, the most obvious one was their new second car.

"I can't do without my car, Jonathan," Helen protested.

Jonathan looked hurt and guilty. He didn't want to deprive his wife of anything she wanted, but they both realised that drastic action was necessary. By deciding to sell the car and Jonathan's coin collection, the Thompsons cut their indebtedness and began to use the amount of the car loan repayment to reduce some of their other debts.

There is an important lesson in what they did. They had to change their perspective on their possessions. Your attitude toward things will determine your success in working your way out of debt. Don't think about how much you will lose or what you paid for the item you are selling. Think about how much you will gain that can reduce your debt immediately.

4. List your liabilities – everything you owe

Many people, particularly if they owe a lot of money, do not know exactly what they owe. However, you must list your debts to get an accurate picture of your current financial situation. You also need to list the interest rate your creditors are charging for each debt.

Debt list – what is owed

	Amount owed	Monthly payment	Interest rate
Mortgage			
Credit cards			
Bank overdraft			
Loans			
Student loans			
Loans from relatives			
Hire purchase, leasing etc			
Business loans			
Others e.g catalogues			
Total debts			

If you use spreadsheets, create one with your debts listed in a column and then use the rows for months so that you have a worksheet similar to the table above, but extended to show each month's repayment and the overall repayment. This spreadsheet will give you a plan to follow – often seeing a debt reduction plan gives hope and provides a powerful motivation to implement the plan. If you are experienced in using spreadsheets, then you could set up a number of interlinking spreadsheets with your budget and cash flows using the 'special paste' functionality and prepare a plan that would impress any accountant!

As you analyse the interest rates on your debt list, you will discover that credit costs vary greatly. Listing your debts will help you establish a priority of debt reduction.

5. The snowball strategy

How do you 'snowball' yourself out of debt?

Pay off your smallest credit card debt

Review your credit card debts. In addition to making the minimum payments on all your cards, focus on accelerating the payment of your smallest high-interest credit card first. You will be encouraged as you make progress, finally eliminating that debt

After you pay off the first credit card, apply its payment toward the next smallest one

After the second card is paid off, apply what you were paying on the first and second toward the third smallest credit card, and so forth. That's the snowball strategy in action!

Pay off your smallest consumer debt

After you have paid off all your credit cards, focus on paying off your consumer debts in exactly the same way as you wiped out your plastic. Make the minimum payments on any of your store card debts, but focus on accelerating the payment of your smallest higher-interest store card debt first. Then, after you pay off the first store card debt, apply its payment toward the next smallest one. After the second one is paid off, apply what you were paying on the first and second to pay off the third, and so forth until you have repaid your credit card and store card debts and then you can start on repaying your unsecured and other debts.

6. Consider earning additional income

Many people hold jobs that simply do not produce enough income to meet their outgoings. Furthermore, where income might have been adequate yesterday that may not be the case if costs are beyond income. Two issues are important about earning additional income. First, decide in advance to pay off debts with the added earnings. We tend to spend more than we make, whether we earn much or little. Spending always seems to keep ahead of earning. Second, earn additional income without harming your relationship with the Lord or with your family if you have one. Be creative in looking for jobs and balance the additional income against other factors such as caring for elderly parents or young children and not taking on so much that you wear yourself out or have no time left to share with your partner.

Helen Thompson proved to be an industrious and innovative person. She started a 'mini-nursery' in her home, baby-sitting three children from her neighbourhood during the day while the children's parents worked. The two older Thompson children were also encouraged to baby-sit in the evenings, and they contributed half of their earnings to the family's debt reduction.

These are only some of the many ways to earn additional income to get out of debt more quickly. However, no matter how much additional income you earn, the key is a commitment that the money is applied to the reduction of debt and not to a higher level of spending.

7. Accumulate no new debt

The only way I know to accumulate no additional debt is to pay for everything with cash, a cheque or a debit card at the time of purchase. I do not believe that credit cards are inherently sinful, but they are dangerous. Statistics show that people spend about one-third more when they use credit cards than when they use cash, because they feel they are not really spending money since they are using a plastic card. As one shopper said to another "I like credit cards a lot more than money because they go so much further!"

Before Rhoda and I became intentional about managing money God's way we had credit and store cards which in the case of the latter were all at their maximum limit. Today we use cards to serve us, not vice versa. Our card balances are automatically paid monthly by direct debit. Even though our son, Simon manages his finances well, he has twice suffered a penalty for late payment. When I reminded him that our cards were automatically paid off every month he replied that he had not been told if he could set up that arrangement. At which point I reminded him that 'this is a bit of a game the credit card companies play, it is how they make money – remember they make up the rules so that they win – not you!'

When I analyse the financial situation of people in debt, I use a simple rule of thumb to determine whether credit cards are too dangerous for them. If they do not pay the entire balance due within two months, I encourage them to perform plastic surgery. Any good scissors will do! When teaching on biblical finances I usually have a pair of scissors in my pocket; it is amazing how people enjoy having their cards cut up.

8. Be content with what you have

We live in a culture whose advertising industry has devised powerful, sophisticated methods of persuading the consumer to buy. There is more than £400 billion spent every year on advertising – more than £6,000 for every person. The people employed in the advertising industry know how to make people buy – that's their job and what they are trained to do. I once attended the Disney University in Orlando and was asked, "when inside the park, who do you think Disney is marketing to?" Their answer is 'the children.' Disney does this through creating memories – they even help you frame your pictures in Main Street with their coloured pavements and roads so there is an array of colour in your pictures. Does it work? Well, take my own family and the answer is 'yes.' We took our family to Disney when they were all young and they can all still fondly recall the rides and experiences of those holidays. Now married, my daughter took her husband who had never been to a Disney park, together with their two year old daughter – and they returned with lots of memories and pictures.

Another purpose of advertising is to create discontentment with what we have. The marketing profession knows how to create desires and to heighten our inner wants until they become irresistible perceived needs. We do not have to conform to the ways of this world: when we do, are we able to be transformed by the renewing of our minds? Frequently the message is intended to create discontentment with what we have.

An American company opened a new plant in Central America because labour was plentiful and inexpensive. The opening of the plant proceeded smoothly until the workers at the plant received their first pay cheques. The next day none of the villagers reported for work. Management waited…one, two, three days. Still no villagers came to work. The plant manager went to see the village chief to talk

about the problem. "Why should we continue to work?" the chief asked in
response to the manager's inquiry. "We are satisfied. We have already earned all
the money we need to live on."

The plant stood idle for two months until someone came up with the bright
idea of sending a mail-order catalogue to every villager. Reading the catalogues
created new desires for the villagers. Soon they returned to work, and there has
been no employment problem since then.

Note these three facts:

- The more television you watch, the more you spend
- The more you look at catalogues and magazines, the more you spend
- The more you shop, the more you spend

Our family is evidence of this. When my daughter suddenly wanted a special box of Disney characters, I know she had seen a television commercial. Clearly, limiting our television viewing also limits our wants.

9. Consider a radical change in your lifestyle

A growing number of people have lowered their expenses significantly to get out of debt more quickly. In order to achieve this some have sold their homes and moved to smaller ones, or rented apartments or moved in with family members. Others have sold cars with large monthly payments and have purchased inexpensive used cars for cash. They have temporarily lowered their cost of living to become free from debt.

10. Do not give up!

Recognise from the beginning there will be a hundred reasons why you should quit or delay your efforts to get out of debt. Don't yield to the temptation of not following through on your commitment. Don't stop until you have reached the marvellous goal of debt-free living. Remember, getting out of debt is just plain hard work, but the freedom is worth the struggle.

How do we escape the car debt trap?

Car debt is one of the leading causes of consumer indebtedness. A large proportion of the cars in our nation are financed. The average person keeps his car between three and four years. The average car generally lasts 10 years.

Here is how you can escape the car debt trap.

1. First, decide in advance to keep your car for at least six years.
2. Second, pay off your car loan.
3. Third, continue paying the monthly car payment but into your own savings account.

Then, when you are ready to replace your car, the saved cash plus the past exchange value should be sufficient to buy a good, low-mileage used car without going into debt.

What about the home mortgage?

I would like to challenge you to seek the Lord's direction concerning your mortgage if you own a home. Is it possible that He may want you to pay off everything you owe, including your mortgage? Usually this is a long-term goal because of the size of the average mortgage.

When Ted Kent stayed with us, he challenged us to plan to repay our mortgage early. Now Ted was no financial adviser, he was probably about 70 and had spent most of his life in Africa as a missionary. He loved the Bible and was often used by God to speak into areas of need. His advice came in the early 1980s when the accountancy business was growing and we were helping clients borrow as much as they required and they could borrow for their homes and businesses. In the case of our own finances we worked on our plans and we were able to finally repay our mortgage some 15 years later.

Let's examine the repayment schedule for a home mortgage. Please do not let the size of the mortgage or the rate of interest hinder your thinking. In the chart that follows we assume a £100,000 mortgage at a 7 percent interest rate. It is to be paid over 25 years. The first year of the payment schedule (also known as an amortisation schedule) would look like the following chart.

Payment	Month	Payment	Interest	Principal	Principal balance
1	Jan	706.78	583.33	123.45	99876.55
2	Feb	706.78	582.61	124.17	99752.38
3	Mar	706.78	581.89	124.89	99627.49
4	Apr	706.78	581.16	125.62	99501.87
5	May	706.78	580.43	126.35	99375.52
6	June	706.78	579.69	127.09	99248.43
7	July	706.78	578.95	127.83	99120.60
8	Aug	706.78	578.20	128.58	98992.02
9	Sep	706.78	577.45	129.33	98862.69
10	Oct	706.78	576.70	130.08	98732.61
11	Nov	706.78	575.94	130.84	98601.77
12	Dec	706.78	575.18	131.60	98470.17
Totals for the year		8481.36	6951.53	1529.83	

As you can see, during the early years of the mortgage almost all the payments go to pay the interest. Of a total £8,481.36 in house payments made during the first year, only £1,529.83 went to reducing the loan. In fact, it will be more than 15 years before the principal and the interest portions of the payment equal each other. I don't know about you, but a 25-year goal to pay off my home mortgage doesn't excite me. If this can be reduced to 15 years, then the goal becomes more attainable. There are several ways to pay off the mortgage in half the time.

One method is to reduce the duration of the loan period while another is to take advantage of any permitted increased monthly payment you are allowed to make under your mortgage agreement. Many mortgage agreements allow an additional monthly payment of up to 10 percent.

With the above example the total interest payable over 25 years is £112,033.76. If the monthly payments were increased to £775.30 the loan would be repaid in 20 years. By reducing the payment term by 5 years the total interest would reduce to £86,071.74, a reduction of £25,962.02 or almost 25 percent less. Furthermore, you will no longer have the remaining monthly payments to make, which under the 25 year mortgage would have amounted to £42,406.80.

A second method is to prepay the next month's principal payment in addition to your regular monthly payment of £706.78. If you do this consistently for 15 years you will have paid off the entire mortgage. During the early years, the additional payment is low, but in the later years the extra payment will become substantial. Examine your mortgage to make certain that the mortgage may be prepaid without any penalty. A home mortgage usually allows such prepayment. Let your lender know what you are planning. Not many borrowers prepay their mortgages, so he may be in shock for a while.

For Rhoda and me, this turned into an exciting time as we began to pay off our mortgage. The Lord provided additional funds in an unexpected way, and today we do not owe anyone anything. Elimination of debt allowed me to take time off from my work to study and develop Crown materials. Our living costs are more modest now, because we do not have any debts or house payments. God may have something similar in mind for you.

Investment debt

Should you borrow money to make an investment? I believe it is permissible, but only if you are not personally required to guarantee the repayment of the debt. The investment for which you borrow and any money invested should be the sole collateral for the debt.

There is the possibility of difficult or catastrophic financial events over which you have no control. It is painful to lose your investment, but it is much more serious to jeopardise meeting your needs by risking all your assets on investment debt. This position may appear too conservative; however, many people have lost everything by guaranteeing debt on investments that went sour. I do not, however, believe it is wise or godly to borrow to speculate e.g. on stocks and shares.

With all your investment decisions, taking appropriate and qualified advice is essential.

Business and church debt

I also want to encourage you to pray about becoming debt-free in your business and church. Many are beginning to pay off all business-related debts, and scores of churches are aggressively working toward satisfying their debts.

Debt repayment responsibilities

Some people delay payments in order to use the creditor's money as long as possible. There are seminars that actually teach people to do just that but this is not biblical. Proverbs 3:27–28 reads "do not withhold good from those to whom it is due, when it is in the power of your hand to do *so*. Do not say to your neighbour 'go, and come back, and tomorrow I will give *it*,' when *you have* it with you" (NKJV). Godly people should pay their debts and bills as promptly as they can. We have a policy of trying to pay each personal bill within a week of receiving it, to demonstrate to others that knowing Jesus Christ has made us financially responsible.

Should you use all your savings to pay off debt?

In my opinion it is wise not to deplete all your savings to pay off debt. Maintain a reasonable level of savings to provide for the unexpected. If you apply all your savings against debt and the unexpected does occur, you probably will be forced to incur more debt to fund the emergency.

Bankruptcy

In bankruptcy, a court of law declares a person unable to pay his debts. Depending upon the type of bankruptcy, the court will either allow the debtor to develop a plan to repay his creditors, or the court will distribute his property among the creditors as payment for the debts.

From 2005 to 2008 the Insolvency Service reported sharp increases in the number of bankruptcy and IVA arrangements. Should a godly person declare bankruptcy? The answer is that seeking bankruptcy or an IVA should not be entertained lightly. Psalm 37:21 tells us that "the wicked borrow and do not repay" and this certainly applies to borrowing with no intent or no concerted effort to repay. But the verse cannot possibly rule out debt cancellation when Deuteronomy 15 is considered.

In my opinion bankruptcy is permissible in three circumstances:

- Where a creditor forces a person into bankruptcy
- When the borrower experiences such extreme financial difficulties that there in no option. There are occasions when bankruptcy is the only viable option when the financial challenges become too extreme to reverse. This option needs to be exercised only after all others have explored.

- If the emotional health of the borrower is at stake because of an inability to cope with the pressure of aggressive creditors, bankruptcy can be an option.

For example, if a husband deserts his wife and children, leaving her with business and family debts for which she is responsible, she may not have the resources or income to meet those obligations. The emotional trauma of an unwanted divorce, coupled with harassment from unsympathetic creditors, may be too much for her to bear.

After a person goes through bankruptcy, they should seek counsel from a competent solicitor to determine if it's legally permissible to repay the debt, even though they are not obligated to do so. If it is allowable, they should make every effort to repay the debt. For a large debt, this may be a long-term goal that is largely dependent upon the Lord supernaturally providing the resources.

Guaranteeing the debt of others

The issue of making guarantees is related to debt. A person who guarantees becomes legally responsible for the debt of another. It is just as if you went to the bank, borrowed the money and gave it to your friend or relative who is asking you to act as guarantor.

Research in the US by the Fed-Trade commission reveals that 50 percent of those who guaranteed bank loans ended up making payments. Seventy-five percent of those who guaranteed for finance company loans ended up making payments. Unfortunately, few guarantors plan for default. The casualty rate is so high because the professional lender has analysed the loan and said to himself, *I won't touch this with a 10-foot pole unless I can get someone who is financially responsible to guarantee this loan.*

Fortunately, Scripture speaks very clearly about guaranteeing. Proverbs 17:18 reads "it's poor judgement to guarantee another person's debt or put up security for a friend" (NLT). The words *poor judgement* are better translated *'destitute of mind.'*

A parent often acts as a guarantor for their child's first car, but we decided not to. We want to model for our children the importance of not guaranteeing, and we also want to discourage them from using debt. Instead, we trained them to plan ahead and save for the cash purchase of their first car.

If you want to help your children out give them a gift. Sometimes it is simply not possible to avoid being guarantor. When the daughter of a friend started college the halls of residence insisted on him acting as guarantor as a condition of allocating his daughter a room. In these situations you must put the money aside or budget for a default.

I urge you to use sound judgement and *never guarantee* a liability or become surety for any debt unless, as above, a guarantee is mandatory. If you have guaranteed, Scripture gives you very direct counsel. Proverbs 6:1–5 reads:

My child, if you have put up security for a friend's debt or agreed to guarantee the debt of a stranger – if you have trapped yourself by your agreement and are caught by what you said – follow my advice and save yourself, for you have placed yourself at your friend's mercy. Now swallow your pride; go and beg to have your name erased. Don't put it off; do it now! Don't rest until you do. Save yourself like a gazelle escaping from a hunter, like a bird fleeing from a net.

Proverbs 6:1–5, NLT

Contrast

Society says: You may use debt as often as you wish; buy now and pay later.

Scripture says: The Lord discourages the use of debt because He wants us free to serve Him.

Commitment

Formalise your desire to get out of debt. Then follow the 10 steps to becoming debt-free. Seek the help and counsel of some friends who can hold you accountable to stick to your plan. The value of seeking advice is the subject of the next chapter.

ten
Counsel – a triple-braided cord

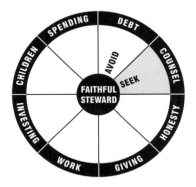

Jonathan and Helen were faced with an uncomfortable decision. Helen's brother and his wife had just moved to Bristol from Surrey. Because they had experienced financial difficulties and been through an Independent Voluntary Arrangement the bank would not lend them the necessary funds for the mortgage unless they had someone to act as guarantor. They asked Jonathan and Helen to find someone. Helen pleaded with Jonathan to do so; however, he was reluctant.

When they came for advice to resolve this problem, I asked them to read the verses from the Bible that addressed guaranteeing. When Helen read the passages she responded "who am I to argue with God? We shouldn't act as guarantors." Jonathan was relieved.

Two are better than one, because they have a good return for their work.

Ecclesiastes 4:9

Two years later, Helen's brother and his wife were divorced and he declared bankruptcy again. Can you imagine the strain on their marriage if they had guaranteed that debt? They would not have been able to survive financially.

Fortunately, they sought counsel. This is a sharp contrast to our culture's practice that says, be a rugged individualist who makes decisions alone and unafraid, coping with any financial pressure in stoic silence.

King Solomon dominated the world scene in his time. Known as the first great commercial king of Israel, he was a skilled diplomat and director of extensive building, shipping and mining ventures. However, Solomon is most often remembered as the wisest king who ever lived. In fact, he made wisdom a subject of study. In Proverbs he wrote "wisdom is more precious than rubies, and nothing you desire can compare with her" (8:11). Solomon's practical recommendations for embracing wisdom are also found in Proverbs: "Get all the advice and instruction you can, so you will be wise the rest of your life" (19:20, NLT). "The way of a fool seems right to him, but a wise man listens to advice" (12:15).

Where should we seek counsel?

The Bible encourages us to seek counsel from several sources.

Scripture

The psalmist wrote "your laws please me; they give me wise advice" (Psalm 119:24, NLT). Moreover, the Bible makes this remarkable claim about itself: "For the word of God is living and active. Sharper than any double-edged sword…it judges the thoughts and attitudes of the heart" (Hebrews 4:12). I have found this to be true. The Bible is a living book that our Lord uses to communicate His direction and truths to all generations. It is the first filter through which we should put our financial decisions. If the Scriptures clearly answer our question, we do not have to go any further because it contains the Lord's written, revealed will. If the Bible is not specific about a particular issue, we should subject our decision to the second source of counsel: godly people.

Godly people

"The mouth of the righteous man utters wisdom, and his tongue speaks what is just. The law of his God is in his heart; his feet do not slip" (Psalm 37:30–31). The apostle Paul recognised the benefit of godly counsel. After he was converted on the Damascus road, he was never alone in his public ministry. He knew and appreciated the value of a couple of extra sets of eyes looking down that straight and narrow road. Timothy, Barnabas, Luke or someone else was always with him.

In fact, in the New Testament *saint* is never used in the singular. It is always in the plural. Someone has described the Christian life as not one of independence from each other but of dependence upon each other. Nowhere is this more clearly illustrated than in Paul's discussion concerning the body of Christ in the 12th chapter of 1 Corinthians. Each of us is pictured as a different part of this body. Our ability to function effectively is dependent upon members working together. In other words, to operate in an optimum way, we need other people to help us. God has given each individual certain abilities and gifts, but God has not given any one person all the skills he or she needs to be most productive.

A person standing alone can be attacked and defeated, but two can stand back-to-back and conquer. Three are even better, for a triple-braided cord is not easily broken.

Ecclesiastes 4:12, NLT

1. Spouse. If you are married, your spouse is to be your primary source of human counsel. A husband and wife are one. Women tend to be gifted with a wonderfully sensitive and intuitive nature that usually is very accurate. Men tend to focus objectively on the facts. A husband and wife need each other to achieve the proper balance for a correct decision. In many relationships one partner is much better at managing personal finance than the other. It is important for the other partner to recognise this but also to work together in managing personal finance. Regardless of your spouse's business education or financial aptitude you must cultivate and seek his or her counsel. You may feel that you have the business background, the financial skills but your partner may have or can develop excellent business and financial skills and their insight will always enrich your own.

I have known bereaved families whose distress has been accentuated by no-one knowing the state of the finances. I have seen families torn apart under the burden of debt that had to be paid after a bread-winning father unexpectedly died. I have also seen families who testify that 'dad has everything in order'; they and their mum are fully provided for. One thing of which we are all certain is death and keeping your spouse involved in home finances is healthy. Normally, there is one spouse who takes the lead responsibility with the other happy to look on. Rhoda and I discuss our budget every month, we review the previous month and look at how we fared compared to the budget. However, I have also known couples who argue about their finances. Discussing household finances in an open, loving and sensitive way and allowing both to be involved in decisions is ultimately an area where the marriage relationship should be made to work well.

Tried it before and it didn't work? Try again, don't give up. One of you might take responsibility for preparing the end of month numbers; let the other person see the figures and then get together to discuss them. Rhoda and I usually spend about 10 minutes going through our finances every month while annually I show her the up-to-date spreadsheet with our finances all laid out. As an accountant I enjoy this sort of thing. Does she 'enjoy' some of these sessions? Not always, but she would not miss out on the involvement she has in the review and planning.

Seeking the counsel of your spouse also helps preserve your relationship because you will both experience the consequences of a decision. If you both agree about a decision, even if it proves to be disastrous, your relationship is more likely to remain intact.

2. Parents. My sons and daughter have all at some time come to us for advice. Since my daughter married she and her husband have approached me once concerning a business opportunity. While I am always there for my children, I do not now expect them to come to me for advice, although they do. We have been blessed with children who have shared their career developments with us, while we are thankful for a son-in-law who loves numbers and planning.

Proverbs 6:20–22 says "my son, keep your father's commands and do not forsake your mother's teaching. . . When you walk, they will guide you; when you sleep, they will watch over you; when you awake, they will speak to you."

In my opinion we should seek their counsel even if they do not yet know Christ or have not been faithful money managers themselves. It is not uncommon for an unspoken barrier to be erected between a child and his parents. Asking their advice is a way to honour them and to build a bridge across any wall.

A word of caution: Genesis 2:24 reads "for this reason a man will leave his father and mother and be united to his wife, and they will become one flesh." Although a husband and wife should seek the counsel of their parents, the advice of the parents should be subordinate to the advice of a spouse, especially if a family conflict materialises.

The Lord

During the process of searching the Bible and obtaining the counsel of godly people, we need to seek direction from the Lord and His Word. In Isaiah 9:6 we are told that one of the Lord's names is 'Wonderful Counsellor.' The Psalms clearly identify the Lord as our counsellor. "I (the Lord) will instruct you and teach you in the way you should go; I will counsel you and watch over you" (Psalm 32:8). "I will praise the Lord, who counsels me" (Psalm 16:7).

We receive the counsel of the Lord by praying and listening. Tell the Lord about your concerns and need for specific direction. Then quietly listen for His still, small voice.

A multitude of counsellors

We should try to obtain advice from a multitude of counsellors. Proverbs 15:22 reads "plans fail for lack of counsel, but with many advisers they succeed." And Proverbs 11:14 says "where there is no counsel, the people fall; but in the multitude of counsellors there is safety" (NKJV).

The older I have become the more I recognise my need for a multitude of counsellors. I had already built three businesses but before starting Crown Financial Ministries in the UK, I sought more counsel than I did for any of my businesses.

Each of us has a limited range of knowledge and experience, and we need others, with their own unique backgrounds, to give us insights and alternatives we never would have considered without their advice.

We should find those who are wise as well as seeking to gain wisdom ourselves. Surrounding yourself with those who are wise can benefit your cheque book whilst also significantly contributing to your emotional and spiritual health. Most people need support at some time in their lives.

Rhoda and I have learned that when someone is subjected to a painful circumstance, it is difficult for him or her to make wise, objective decisions. We have experienced the safety of having a group of people who love one another – even when it hurts. I am more receptive to constructive criticism when it comes from someone I respect, someone who cares for me. Solomon describes the benefits of dependence upon one another in this passage:

Two are better than one, because they have a good reward for their labour. For if they fall, one will lift up his companion. But woe to him who is alone when he falls, for he has no one to help him up....Though one may be overpowered by another, two can withstand him. And a threefold cord is not quickly broken.

Ecclesiastes 4:9–12 NKJV

Big decisions

Because of their importance and permanence, some decisions deserve more attention than others. Decisions concerning a career or a house purchase, for example, affect us for a longer period of time than most other choices we make. Throughout Scripture we are admonished to wait upon the Lord. Whenever you face a major decision or experience a sense of confusion concerning a course of action, I encourage you to set aside some time to pray, fast and listen quietly for His will.

Counsel to avoid

We need to avoid one particular source of counsel. "Blessed is the man who does not walk in the counsel of the wicked" (Psalm 1:1). The word 'blessed' literally means 'happy many times over.' The word 'wicked' is a strong word and is often used to describe people who behave in an extremely cruel manner. The former Iraqi dictator was often described by the media as wicked. However, the dictionary widens the use of the term to include those who are sinful or iniquitous, while the first three synonyms on dictionary.com are unrighteous, ungodly and godless.

There are people who would advise us to do things that are wrong or would take advantage of us in financial matters for their advantage. We need discernment. If anything sounds too good to be true it probably is!

In my opinion, if there is no suitably qualified Christian, then technical or professional advice should be sought from those you deem to be qualified to advise. Armed with that advice, our financial decision should be based on prayer and possibly a second opinion from those who know the Lord.

Never seek the counsel of fortune tellers or mediums

The Bible bluntly tells us never to seek the advice of fortune tellers, mediums or spiritualists: "Do not turn to mediums or seek out spiritualists, for you will be defiled by them. I am the Lord your God" (Leviticus 19:31). Study this next passage carefully: "Saul died because he was unfaithful to the Lord…and even consulted a medium for guidance, and did not enquire of the Lord. So the Lord put him to death" (1 Chronicles 10:13 – 14).

Saul died, in part, because he went to a medium. We should also avoid any methods they use in forecasting the future, such as horoscopes, ouija boards, tarot cards and all other practices of the occult.

Be careful of the biased

We need to be cautious of the counsel of biased people. When receiving financial advice, ask yourself this question: *What stake does this person have in the outcome of my decision?* If the adviser will profit, always seek a second unbiased opinion.

Contrast

Society says: Be your own person; stand on your own two feet. You don't need anyone to tell you what to do.

Scripture says: "The Counsellor, the Holy Spirit whom the Father will send in my name, will teach you all things and will remind you of everything I have said to you" (John 14:26).

Commitment

In my experience, the vast majority of those in financial difficulties have not followed the scriptural principle of seeking wise counsel. They have been moulded by our culture's view that admitting a need and asking for advice is only for those who are not strong enough to be self-sufficient.

More often than not, a person's pride is the biggest deterrent to seeking advice. This is especially true in a financial crisis. It is embarrassing to expose our problems to someone else.

Another reason for reluctance to seek counsel is the fear that an objective evaluation of our finances may bring to the surface issues we would rather avoid: a lack of disciplined spending, an unrealistic budget, a lack of communication in the family or a suggestion to give up something dear to us.

I cannot overemphasise the importance of counsel, and I encourage you to evaluate your situation. If you do not have a counsellor, try to cultivate a friendship with at least one godly person who can advise you.

eleven
Honesty – absolutely

One evening I received a phone call I will never forget. It was from Jonathan Thompson. "You won't believe what just happened to me!" he said. "I went to fill up my tank and bought £30 worth of petrol. I asked the attendant for a receipt and he made it out for £50. When I pointed out the mistake, the attendant replied "oh, just record that in your books, and you'll get the cash out of your company and the tax relief. It's what everyone asks me to do."

Like Jonathan, all of us – the executive, the employee and the homemaker – have to make daily decisions about whether or not to handle money honestly. Do you tell the cashier at the grocery store when you receive too much change? Have you ever tried to sell something and been tempted not to tell the whole truth because you might lose a sale?

Honesty in society

News reports inform us of how politicians sometimes make false expense claims while some television companies admit to being dishonest with their handling of money from calls to reality TV programmes and viewer competitions. When our politicians and media are tainted then it is seemingly inevitable that others will think nothing of following suit. With companies being accused of price fixing and a host of other 'dishonest' arrangements being exposed, standards plummet because the example set by those in power is often perceived to be a sort of benchmark of what you can 'get away with.'

One day as I left my office and went into the local shop, I saw three young lads stealing. They saw me and ran out of the shop. I decided to apprehend them and succeeded in catching two of them. I duly hauled them back to the shop – much to the annoyance of the shopkeeper who was not interested in the slightest. I decided to administer my own admonition and threat of calling the police before dismissing them. I figured that if I did not give them a good telling off they might repeat the act – only next time it could be a more serious.

> *Every man did what was right in his own eyes.*
>
> **Judges 17:6, AMP**

So, how about what we help ourselves to from the workplace – those little things like stationery, or materials from production? Are there any areas where you are or have been dishonest? How about working a full day? How about taking time off and reporting it as sickness? Or the inflated expenses account?

We should not adopt the attitude that 'it's okay, the way the economy is going you've got to be shrewd just to survive.' Or 'the company doesn't need it, and besides everyone does it.' We live in an age of 'relative honesty' in which people formulate their own standards of honesty which change with the circumstances. The Bible speaks of a similar time which was a turbulent period in Israel's history. "Everyone did as he saw fit" (Judges 17:6).

Honesty in scripture

Relative honesty contrasts sharply with the standard that we find in Scripture. God demands absolute honesty. Proverbs 20:23 reads "the Lord detests differing weights, and dishonest scales do not please him." And Proverbs 12:22 states "lying lips *are* an abomination to the Lord" (NKJV). Leviticus 19:11 says "do not steal. Do not lie. Do not deceive one another." Study this comparison between what the Scriptures teach and what our society practices concerning honesty.

Issue	Scripture	Society
Standard of honesty:	Complete honesty	Changes with circumstances
God's concern about honesty:	He requires it	There is no God or He looks the other way
The decision to be honest or dishonest is based upon:	Faith in the invisible, living God	Only the facts that can be seen
Question usually asked deciding whether to be honest:	Will it please God?	Will I get away with it?

The God of truth

Truthfulness is one of God's attributes. "I am...the truth" (John 14:6). Moreover, He commands us to reflect His honest and holy character: "Be holy in all you do; for it is written: 'Be holy, because I am holy'" (1 Peter 1:15–16). God's nature is in stark contrast to Satan's nature. John 8:44 describes the devil's character: "(The devil)...there is no truth in him. When he lies, he speaks his native language, for he is a liar and the father of lies." The Lord wants us to become conformed to His honest character rather than to the dishonest nature of the devil.

Why does God demand absolute honesty?

God has imposed the standard of absolute honesty for five reasons.

1. We cannot practice dishonesty and love God

When we practice dishonesty, we are acting as if the living God does not exist, and it is impossible to love God if He doesn't exist. Stop and think about what we are saying when we make a decision to be dishonest:

- God is not able to provide exactly what I need – even though He has promised to do so (Matthew 6:33). I will take things into my own hands and do them my own dishonest way
- God is incapable of discovering my dishonesty
- God is powerless to discipline me

If we really believed that God would discipline us, then we would not consider acting dishonestly.

Honest behaviour is an issue of faith. An honest decision may look foolish in light of the circumstances we can observe. However, a godly person has mastered the art of considering another factor which is valid, even though invisible: the person of Jesus Christ. Every honest decision strengthens our faith in the living God. However, if we choose to be dishonest, we essentially deny the existence of the Lord. Scripture declares that those who practice dishonesty hate God: "He whose walk is upright fears the Lord, but he whose ways are devious despises him" (Proverbs 14:2).

2. We cannot practice dishonesty and love our neighbour

The Lord demands absolute honesty because dishonest behaviour violates the second commandment "you shall love your neighbour as yourself" (Mark 12:31, NKJV). Romans 13:9–10 reads "love your neighbour as yourself. Love does no harm to its neighbour."

When we act dishonestly, we are stealing from another person. We may fool ourselves into thinking it is a business the government or an insurance company that is suffering loss, but if we look at the bottom line, it is the business owners or fellow taxpayers or policyholders from whom we are stealing. It is just as if we took the money from their wallets. We need to remember that dishonesty always injures people.

3. Honesty creates credibility for evangelism

Our Lord demands that we be absolutely honest in order to demonstrate the reality of Jesus Christ to those who do not yet know Him. Our actions speak louder than our words. Scripture says that we should "Become blameless and pure, children of God without fault in a crooked and depraved generation, in which you shine like stars in the universe" (Philippians 2:15).

Roger Downes, a home owner, had been planning an extension to his home for some time. Finally he and his wife contacted two builders for quotations. The first builder came round and after looking at the plans said his goodbye and told Roger that he would email a quote to him next week. The next builder also looked at the plans and asked Roger if anyone else was quoting. 'Yes' said Roger. The builder checked what Roger did for a living (checking he did not work for HM Revenue & Customs) and then offered to do the extension at 20 percent less than any other quotation provided the job was cash so that no VAT would be charged.

Roger was tempted, but knew it would be wrong. He responded, "I'm sorry, I can't do that because I am a Christian and I cannot be involved in something that is dishonest."

"You should have seen the look on the builder's face," Roger said, "he almost went into shock." Then an interesting thing happened. The builder returned three days later to apologise for what he had said and asked Roger what was so important to him when he could have saved thousands of pounds. That was Roger's chance to share his faith and invite the builder to church.

Honest behaviour confirms to those who do not yet know Him that we serve a holy God.

4. Honesty confirms God's direction

Proverbs 4:24–26 reads "put away perversity from your mouth; keep corrupt talk far from your lips. Let your eyes look straight ahead....Make level paths for your feet and take only ways that are firm."

What a tremendous principle! As you are absolutely honest, *all your ways will be established.*" Choosing to walk the narrow path of honesty eliminates the many possible avenues of dishonesty. Decision-making becomes simpler because the honest path is a clear path.

"If only I'd understood this," Dan said as tears streamed down his cheeks.

"Lucy and I wanted that house so much. It was our dream home, but our debts were so large that we couldn't qualify for the mortgage. The only way we could buy the house was to hide some of our debts from the bank. It was the worst decision of our lives. Almost immediately we were unable to meet the mortgage payment and pay our other debts too. The pressure built. It was almost more than Lucy could stand. Our dream house ended up causing a family nightmare. I not only lost the home, but I nearly lost my wife."

Had Dan and Lucy been honest, the bank would not have approved the loan. They would not have been able to purchase that particular home. If they had prayed and waited, perhaps the Lord would have brought them something more affordable, thus avoiding the pressure that almost ended their marriage. Honesty helps confirm God's direction.

5. Even a small act of dishonesty is devastating

God requires us to be *absolutely honest* because even the smallest act of dishonesty is sin. Even the smallest 'white lie' can harden our hearts and make our consciences increasingly insensitive to sin. This can deafen our ears to the still, small voice of the Lord. A single cancer cell of small dishonesty can multiply and spread to greater dishonesty. "Whoever is dishonest with very little will also be dishonest with much" (Luke 16:10).

It was an event in Abraham's life that challenged him to be honest in small matters. The king of Sodom offered Abraham all the goods he recovered when he returned from successfully rescuing the people of Sodom. Abraham answered the king, "I have raised my hand to the Lord… that I will accept nothing belonging to you" (Genesis 14:22–23).

Just as Abraham was unwilling to take so much as a thread or a sandal thong, I challenge you to make a similar commitment in this area of honesty. Promise (or make a covenant) not to steal a stamp, or a photocopy, or a paper clip, or a long-distance telephone call, or a penny from your employer, the government or anyone else. The people of God must be honest in even the smallest, seemingly inconsequential matters.

How do we escape the temptation of dishonesty?

Unless we deny ourselves and live our lives yielded to the Holy Spirit, all of us will be dishonest. "Live by the Spirit, and you will not gratify the desires of the sinful nature" (Galatians 5:16). The desire of our human nature is to act dishonestly. "Out of men's hearts, come evil thoughts…theft…deceit" (Mark 7:21–22). The desire of the Spirit is for us to be absolutely honest. I can't overemphasise that the life of absolute honesty is supernatural. We must submit ourselves entirely to Christ as Lord and allow Him to live His life through us.

Maintain a healthy fear of the Lord

Proverbs 16:6 reads "through the fear of the Lord a man avoids evil." A 'healthy fear' of the Lord does not mean that we have to view God as a big bully just waiting for the opportunity to punish us; rather, He is a loving Father who, out of infinite love, disciplines His children for their benefit. "God disciplines us for our good, that we may share in his holiness"

(Hebrews 12:10).

Howard once shared a hotel room with a friend during a business trip. As they were leaving, his friend slipped one of the hotel's drinking glasses into his pocket and walked to the car. Howard was overwhelmed by the fear of the Lord. He tells me that it was difficult to explain how he felt. The closest description he's found is in Daniel 5:6, which records the Babylonian king's reaction to the handwriting on the wall: "The king's....thoughts troubled him, so that the joints of his hips were loosened and his knees knocked against each other" (NKJV).

There Howard was with his knees knocking as he thought of Hebrews 12:11, "No discipline seems pleasant at the time, but painful. Later on, however, it produces a harvest of righteousness and peace for those who have been trained by it." Discipline hurts! Given the choice, he would rather *"share His holiness"* out of obedience to His Word than to make a deliberate decision that would prompt his loving Father to discipline him. "I can't tell you how relieved I was when my friend returned the glass after I pleaded with him to do so!" said Howard.

By a loss of property

I believe that our heavenly Father will not allow us to keep anything we have acquired dishonestly. Proverbs 13:11 reads, "Dishonest money dwindles away."

Linda purchased four azalea plants, but the sales cashier had only charged her for one. She knew it, but she left the garden centre anyway without paying for the other three. She said it was simply miraculous how quickly three of those four plants died.

Think about this for a moment: If you are a parent and your child steals something, do you allow the child to keep it? Of course not. You require its return because the child's character would be damaged if he kept the stolen property. Not only do you insist upon its return, but you probably want the child to experience enough discomfort to produce a lasting impression. For example, you might have the child confess the theft and ask forgiveness from the shop manager. When our heavenly Father lovingly disciplines us, it usually is done in such a way that we will not forget.

What to do when we have been dishonest?

Unfortunately, all of us are dishonest from time to time. Once we recognise that we have acted dishonestly, we need to do three things:

1. Restore our fellowship with God

Anytime we sin, our fellowship with the Lord is broken. This needs to be restored. First John 1:9 tells us how: "If we confess our sins, he is faithful and just and will forgive us our sins and purify us from all unrighteousness." We must agree with God that our dishonesty is sin and then accept His gracious forgiveness so we can again enjoy His fellowship.

2. Restore our fellowship with people

We need to confess our dishonesty to the person we offended. "Confess your sins to each other" (James 5:16). This has been difficult for me. After years of avoiding this step, I have started confessing my dishonesty to others. A person's lack of financial prosperity may be a consequence of violating this principle. "He who conceals his sins does not prosper, but whoever confesses and renounces them finds mercy" (Proverbs 28:13).

3. Restore dishonestly acquired property

If we have acquired anything dishonestly, we must return it to its rightful owner: "when he thus sins and becomes guilty, he must return what he has stolen or taken by extortion…or whatever it was he swore falsely about. He must make restitution in full, add a fifth of the value to it and give it all to the owner on the day" (Leviticus 6:4–5).

Restitution is a tangible expression of repentance and an effort to correct a wrong. If it's not possible for restitution to be made to the injured party, then the property should be given to the Lord. Numbers 5:8 teaches "but if that person has no close relative to whom restitution can be made for the wrong, the restitution belongs to the Lord and must be given to the priest."

Bribes

A bribe is defined as 'money or any other valuable consideration given or promised with a view to corrupting the behaviour of a person.'

Taking a bribe is clearly prohibited by Scripture: "Do not accept a bribe, for a bribe blinds those who see and twists the words of the righteous" (Exodus 23:8). Bribes are sometimes subtly disguised as a 'gift' or 'referral fee.' Evaluate any such offer to confirm that it is not in reality a bribe.

Blessings and curses

Listed below are some of the blessings the Lord has promised for the honest and some of the curses reserved for the dishonest. Read these slowly and prayerfully and ask God to use His Word to motivate you to a life of honesty.

Blessings promised for the honest

- **Intimacy with the Lord:** "For the Lord detests a perverse man but takes the upright into his confidence" (Proverbs 3:32).
- **A blessed family:** "The righteous man leads a blameless life; blessed are his children after him" (Proverbs 20:7).
- **Long life:** "Truthful lips endure for ever, but a lying tongue lasts only a moment" (Proverbs 12:19).
- **Prosperity:** "The house of the righteous contains great treasure, but the income of the wicked brings them trouble" (Proverbs 15:6).

Curses reserved for the dishonest

- **Alienation from God:** "For the Lord detests a perverse man but takes the upright into his confidence" (Proverbs 3:32).
- **Family problems:** "A greedy man brings trouble to his family, but he who hates bribes will live" (Proverbs 15:27).
- **Death:** "A fortune made by a lying tongue is a fleeting vapour and a deadly snare" (Proverbs 21:6).
- **Poverty:** "Dishonest money dwindles away " (Proverbs 13:11).

Are you the person the Lord is looking for?

I believe we seriously underestimate the impact that *one* honest person can have. Read Jeremiah 5:1 carefully: "go up and down the streets of Jerusalem, look around and consider, search through her squares. If you can find but one person who deals honestly and seeks the truth, I (the Lord) will forgive this city." The destiny of an entire city hung in the balance. Its future depended upon there being one absolutely honest person. Will you be that person for your community? You may not receive the acclaim of the media, the business community or politicians, but in God's economy, your commitment to honesty can have an influence on your city.

Contrast

Society says: You can be dishonest because everyone else is.

Scripture says: The Lord demands absolute honesty in even the smallest matters.

Commitment

Prayerfully review this checklist for honest behaviour:

1. Do I report all income on my tax returns, and are all my tax and expense claims legitimate?
2. Do I care for the property of others as if it were my own?
3. Do I have the habit of telling "little white lies?"
4. Do I ever misappropriate materials, office supplies, stamps or anything else that belongs to my employer?
5. If I am undercharged on a purchase, do I report it?
6. Do I look out for the interests of others as well as my own?

Ask God to show you any other dishonest behaviour that should be changed, especially in the grey areas. Ask a close friend to encourage you and to hold you accountable to be honest.

twelve
Giving –
what is your attitude

Jonathan and Helen decided to enrol in a Crown Financial Ministries small group study to learn what the Scriptures teach about money. A couple of months after the group started, I met Jonathan for breakfast. He told me how much the study meant to him, and then sheepishly confessed "I've never had any desire to give money. Now that I understand what the Bible has to say about it, I want to give but I'm frustrated. How can I possibly

> *It is more blessed to give than to receive.*
>
> **Jesus Christ**
> **From Acts 20:35**

decide where to give? It seems there are so many good causes and so many needs that I could help meet. I feel guilty that perhaps we're not giving enough. And sometimes I become cynical because I feel I'm manipulated subtly by people whose goals may be worthwhile but whose means of achieving those goals are questionable."

I knew what Jonathan was experiencing. I used to be as frustrated as he was. Since learning what Scripture says about giving, the Holy Spirit has been changing my attitudes, and I have experienced the blessings of giving. Indeed, giving has been the most liberating area in my Christian experience.

The Old and New Testaments place a great deal of emphasis on giving.

In fact, there are more verses related to giving than any other subject on money. There are many commands, practical suggestions, examples and exhortations concerning this facet of stewardship. Everywhere in the Bible covetousness and greed are condemned, and generosity and charity are encouraged.

Attitude in giving

Giving with the proper attitude is crucial. Paul writes in 1 Corinthians 13:3, "If I give all I possess to the poor…but have not love, I gain nothing." It is hard to imagine anything more commendable than giving everything to the poor. But if it is done with the wrong attitude, without love, it is of no benefit to the giver. The Lord set the example of giving motivated by love. "For God so *loved* the world that he *gave* his one and only Son" (John 3:16, italics added). Note the sequence: Because God loved, He gave.

I struggled for years to give consistently out of a heart of love. I believe the only way to do this is to recognise that each gift is actually given to the Lord Himself. An example of this perspective is found in Numbers 18:24: "I give to the Levites as their inheritance the tithes that the Israelites present *as* an offering to the Lord" (NKJV).

If giving is simply giving to our church, to a ministry, a charitable organisation or to a needy person it is charity and that is no bad thing in itself. But when our giving is first to the Lord it becomes an act of worship. Because Jesus Christ is our Creator, our Saviour and our faithful Provider, we can express our gratefulness and love by giving our gifts to Him. For example, when the offering plate is being passed at church, we should consciously remind ourselves that we are giving our gifts to the Lord Himself.

Stop and examine yourself. What is your attitude toward giving? I cannot stress too much the importance of giving with the proper attitude.

Advantages of giving

Of course, a gift benefits the recipient, but according to God's economy, if a gift is given with the proper attitude, the giver benefits more than the receiver. "Remember the words of the Lord Jesus, that He said 'it is more blessed to give than to receive'" (Acts 20:35 NKJV). As we examine Scripture, we find the giver benefits in four significant areas.

1. Increase in intimacy

Above all else, giving directs our attention and hearts to Christ. Matthew 6:21 tells us "for where your treasure is, there your heart will be also." This is why it is so necessary to go through the process of consciously giving each gift to the person of Jesus Christ. When you give your gift to Him, your heart will automatically be drawn to the Lord.

2. Development of character

Our heavenly Father wants us, as His children, to be conformed to the image of His Son. The character of Christ is unselfish. Unfortunately, humans are by nature selfish. One of the key ways our character becomes conformed to Christ is by habitual giving. Someone once said "giving is not God's way of raising money; it is God's way of raising people into the likeness of His Son." John Wesley, also based in Bristol for many years, said "money never stays with me. It would burn if it did. I throw it out of my hands as soon as possible, lest it should find its way to my heart." The Lord understands that for us to develop into the people He wants us to be, we must learn how to share our possessions freely. If we don't, our inbred selfishness will grow and dominate us."

An extreme example is Howard Hughes, whose story was retold in the film 'The Aviator.' In his youth Hughes was a typical playboy with a passion for parties and beautiful women and an aversion toward giving. As he grew older and turned an inheritance into a vast fortune, he became more and more tight fisted. He let his wealth create an ever-increasing barrier between himself and other people. In his last years he lived in seclusion and became a recluse whose life was devoted to avoiding germs and people."

George Müeller whose orphanage homes were based in my home city of Bristol is a sharp contrast to Hughes. Müeller also inherited wealth, but unlike Hughes, he established a life-long pattern of generous sharing. His life was characterised by serving the needs of others. Sharing leads to life itself. It is the most effective antidote to the human disease of covetousness. "Command them…to be rich in good deeds, and to be generous and willing to share…so that they may take hold of the life that is truly life"(1 Timothy 6:18–19).

3. Treasures in Heaven

Matthew 6:20 reads "but store up for yourselves treasures in heaven, where moth and rust do not destroy, and where thieves do not break in and steal." The Lord tells us that there really is something akin to the "Royal Bank of Heaven." He wants us to know that we can invest for eternity.

Paul wrote "not that I am looking for a gift, but I am looking for what may be credited to your account" (Philippians 4:17). A spiritual account exists for each of us in heaven. We will be privileged to enjoy it forever. We 'can't take it with us,' but we can make deposits to our heavenly account before we die.

The Bible is full of God's promises to His faithful children. Rewards both now and forever are in store for those who love and obey Him. Giving results in a material increase.

So God can choose to bless our giving in this world with increased material possessions. But what if He does not? Most of the verses about eternal rewards do not mention money or possessions as rewards for giving. Instead they mention rewards in heaven. These seem to fall into three main categories:

Crowns: 2 Timothy 4:8 "Now there is in store for me the crown of righteousness, which the Lord, the righteous Judge, will award to me on that day – and not only to me, but also to all who have longed for his appearing." See also James 1:12; 1 Peter 5:4 and Revelation 2:10.

Treasure: Luke 12:33 "Sell your possessions and give to the poor. Provide purses for yourselves that will not wear out, a treasure in heaven that will not be exhausted, where no thief comes near and no moth destroys." See also Matthew 6:20; Mark 10:21 and 1 Timothy 6:19.

Positions of authority: 2 Timothy 2:12 12 "If we endure, we will also reign with him." Also see Matthew 19:28 and Revelation 3:21.Though we will not know for sure what each of these rewards will be like until we reach heaven, the emphasis placed on obtaining them should make us excited about the prospect.

4. Increase on earth

Giving with the proper attitude also results in a material increase flowing to the giver. Proverbs 11:24–25 informs us "one man gives freely, yet gains even more; another withholds unduly, but comes to poverty. A generous man will prosper; he who refreshes others will himself be refreshed."

Examine 2 Corinthians 9:6 and 8: "Whoever sows sparingly will also reap sparingly, and whoever sows generously will also reap generously.

God is able to make all grace abound to you…that you will abound in every good work."

These verses teach that giving results in a material increase, however, I need to sound two notes of caution at this point lest I am misunderstood. Giving is not the key that unlocks personal prosperity. To give in order to receive contradicts the importance of attitude mentioned earlier. Remember also that material prosperity was far from the experience both of the Macedonian church that Paul commended to the Corinthians (2 Cor. 8:1-2) and the Jerusalem church for whom Paul was organising the collection. Paul himself knew times of hardship alongside plenty and he reminds the church at Corinth that few had social or economic standing when they were called. Of course Jesus himself had few possessions and depended on others for his physical needs. What seems certain is that generosity will never impoverish us either spiritually or financially.

Thomas Gouge, a noted minister in the 1600s said:

I dare challenge all the world to give me one instance, or at least any considerable number of instances of any truly merciful men, whose charity has undone them. But as living wells the more they are drawn, the more freely they spring and flow; so the substance of liberal men doth oftentimes, if not, ordinarily, multiply in the very distribution: even as the five loaves and few fishes did multiply in their distribution by the hands of the Redeemer. And the widow's oil increased by pouring it out for the holy prophet.

Reverend Gouge personally lived out this testimony as he funded his own ministry as well as many poor people in his area using the estate left by his father.

Secondly, note carefully why the Lord returns an increase materially: *"That…you may have an abundance for every good deed."* As shown in the diagram on the next page, the Lord produces an increase so that we may give more and have our needs met at the same time.

However, there are also many examples in Scripture of God's current blessings. Much of the reward for giving that was promised in the Old Testament related to increased crops and herds as well as protection from enemies – all of which relate to physical rewards during life on earth.

The amount to give

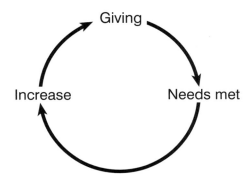

Let's survey what the Scriptures say about how much to give. Under the Old Testament a tithe, or 10 percent of a person's earnings, was required to be given. When the children of Israel disobeyed this commandment, it was regarded as robbing God Himself. Listen to these solemn words in Malachi's days: "Should people cheat God? Yet you have cheated me! But you ask 'What do you mean? When did we ever cheat you?' You have cheated me of the tithes and offerings due to me. You are under a curse, for your whole nation has been cheating me " (Malachi 3:8-9, NLT).

In addition to the tithe, the Hebrews were to give offerings. Furthermore, the Lord made special provisions for the needs of the poor. For example, every seven years all debts were cancelled, and special rules governed harvesting so that the poor could gather food.

In the New Testament the tithe is neither specifically rejected nor specifically recommended. It does teach us to give in proportion to the material blessing we have received, and it especially commends sacrificial giving. In the New Testament all the examples of giving show amounts of much more than 10 percent.

What I like about the tithe or any fixed percentage of giving is that it is systematic, and the amount of the gift is easy to compute. The danger of the tithe is that it can be treated simply as another bill to be paid. By not giving out of a heart of love, I place myself in a position where I cannot receive the blessings the Lord has designed for a giver. Another potential danger of tithing is the view that once I have tithed, I have fulfilled all my obligations to give. For many Christians the tithe should be the beginning of their giving, not the full extent.

Scripture is unclear on exactly how much we should give. I believe this lack of clarity is because the decision concerning the amount an individual gives should be based on a personal relationship with God. As we seek the guidance of the Spirit through an active prayer life, giving suddenly becomes an exciting adventure.

Howard told me about his time with the Abernathy family. They used to own a shoe and leather business. The members of the family had been praying that God would direct their sharing. As they prayed, they were impressed with the needs of the Wilsons, a large family in their community. Finances were tight for the Wilsons because the school year was starting. The Johnsons decided to give each of the five Wilson children two pairs of shoes. They did not know that the shoes had been precisely what the Khan children had been praying for.

Around the dinner table one evening the Wilson children again prayed for shoes. After they had finished praying, their mother said, "You don't have to ask the Lord for shoes anymore. God has answered your prayers." One by one the shoes were brought out.

By the time it was over, the children thought God was in the shoe business! Howard said, "Mark, I wish you could have seen the sense of awe on the faces of the Johnsons as they experienced firsthand how God was directing their sharing through the quiet mystery of prayer."

How much should you give?

To answer this question, first submit yourself to God. Earnestly seek His will for you. "And they did do as we expected, but they gave themselves first to the Lord and then to us in keeping with God's Will" (2 Corinthians 8:5).

Rhoda and I have given a great deal of thought and prayer to the question of how much we should share. We have concluded that the tithe is the minimum amount we should give. Then, we give over and above the tithe as God prospers or directs.

The pattern of giving

During Paul's third missionary journey he wrote to the Corinthians concerning a promised collection to meet the needs of the persecuted believers in Jerusalem. "On the first day of every week, each one of you should set aside a sum of money in keeping with his income, saving it up, so that when I come no collections will have to be made." (1 Corinthians 16:2). His comments provide practical instruction about giving. Let's call this pattern 'Paul's Pod of Ps' – giving that is personal, out of a periodic, private deposit and premeditated.

Giving should be personal

Giving is the privilege and responsibility of every Christian, young and old, rich and poor. *"Let each one of you...."* The benefits of giving are intended for each person to enjoy.

Several years ago Howard met a neighbour who loved to give. It was immediately apparent to him that he gained great pleasure from giving. Howard had never met a person like that before. As their relationship grew, Howard discovered how he learned to be a joyful giver. His parents shared generously with those in need and required each of their children to establish this habit. As a consequence, he continues to enjoy a level of freedom in sharing that few people experience.

Giving should be periodic

Periodic is the second of Paul's Ps. The Lord understands that we need to give regularly, *"on the first day of every week."* Giving regularly helps draw us consistently to Christ.

Giving should be out of a private deposit

"Put aside and save...." If you experience difficulty in monitoring the money you have decided to give, consider opening a separate bank account. Rhoda and I call it the 'Lord's account'. You might also do something as simple as setting aside a special 'giving jar' into which you deposit the money you intend to give.

The most gratifying part of setting aside money has been the thrill of praying that God would make us aware of needs and then enable us to respond.

Giving should be premeditated

Almost every Sunday after he became a Christian, Bev would ask Howard, "Darling how much would you like to give this week at church?" His standard reply was "I don't care. You make that decision." Because of his cavalier attitude, he was not in a position to experience the blessing meant for the giver. To know the full joy and reap the blessing of giving, it must not be done carelessly. "Each man should give what he has decided in his heart to give, not reluctantly or under compulsion, for God loves a cheerful giver" (2 Corinthians 9:7). Our giving should involve thought, planning and prayer. However, many believers operate like Howard used to – never thinking about giving until it is time for the offering.

The supreme example of premeditated giving was set by our Saviour, "who for the joy set before Him endured the cross" (Hebrews 12:2).

To whom do we give?

We are told to share and provide for three categories of people. With whom and in what proportion one gives varies with the needs God lays on the heart of each believer.

1. Providing for dependents
In our culture we are experiencing a tragic breakdown in this area of sharing. Husbands have failed to provide for their wives, parents have neglected their children, and grown sons and daughters have forsaken their elderly parents. Such neglect is solemnly condemned. "If anyone does not provide for his relatives, and especially for his immediate family, he has denied the faith and is worse than an unbeliever" (1 Timothy 5:8). Meeting the needs of your family is the first priority in sharing and one in which there should be no compromise.

2. The local church, Christian workers and ministries
Throughout its pages, the Bible focuses on supporting the Lord's ministry. The Old Testament priesthood was to receive specific support (Numbers 18:21), and the New Testament teaching on ministry support is just as strong. "The elders who direct the affairs of the church well are worthy of double honour, especially those whose work is preaching and teaching" (1 Timothy 5:17). How many Christian workers have been distracted from their ministry by inadequate support? Far too many.

People ask if we should give only through our local church. In our case, the answer is no. However, we do give a minimum of 10 percent of our regular income through our church because we believe this is a tangible expression of our commitment to our church. But we also give to others who are directly having an influence on us. "Anyone who receives instruction in the word must share all good things with his instructor" (Galatians 6:6).

3. The poor

I didn't go to bed hungry last night, but conservative estimates are that 800 million people – that's more than 12 percent of the world's people – go to bed hungry each night. That is overwhelming. The number is so great that it may leave us feeling hopeless about what we can do. But Scripture consistently emphasises our responsibility to give to the poor and the destitute.

In Matthew 25:34–45 we are confronted with one of the most exciting yet sobering truths in the Bible. Read this passage carefully:

"Then the King will say… 'For I was hungry and you gave me something to eat, I was thirsty and you gave me something to drink'.…Then the righteous will answer him, 'Lord, when did we see you hungry and feed you, or thirsty and give you something to drink?' The King will reply, 'I tell you the truth, whatever you did for one of the least of these brothers of mine, you did for me.' Then he will say to those on his left, 'Depart from me, you who are cursed, into the eternal fire …for I was hungry and you gave me nothing to eat, I was thirsty and you gave me nothing to drink…whatever you did not do for one of the least of these, you did not do for me.'"

Matthew 25:34–45

In some mysterious way that we cannot fully comprehend, Jesus personally identifies with the poor. Do you want to minister to Christ? You do so when you give to the poor. If that truth is staggering, then the opposite is terrifying. When we do not give to the poor, we leave Christ Himself hungry and thirsty.

Three areas of our Christian life are affected by our giving or our lack of giving to the poor:

1. Prayer

A lack of giving to the poor could be the cause of unanswered prayer. "Is not this the kind of fasting I have chosen. . . is it not to share your food with the hungry and to provide the poor wanderer with shelter…then you will call, and the Lord will answer" (Isaiah 58:6–9). And "if a man shuts his ears to the cry of the poor, he too will cry out and not be answered" (Proverbs 21:13).

2. Provision

Our provision is conditioned upon our giving to the needy. "He who gives to the poor will not lack, but he who hides his eyes will have many curses" (Proverbs 28:27NKJ).

3. Knowing Jesus Christ intimately

One who does not give to the poor does not know the Lord intimately. "He judged the cause of the poor and needy; then *it was* well. *Was* not this knowing Me? says the Lord" (Jeremiah 22:16 NKJV).

With household budgets stretched and consumerism having such a stranglehold, there often seems no place for giving to the poor. Nor should we assume that with the work of Government agencies and the commitment of many excellent charities that the poor are provided for. It was always God's intention that his people should be responsible for helping the poor and around the country churches are doing just that. A friend's church supports a maternity hospital in Shyira, Rwanda and this initiative has received much support from the wider community. Other churches send practical support to Romania, support relief workers in Africa and much, much more. The passages just cited and the ministry of Jesus are evidence that giving must include giving to the poor. The first instinct of Zacchaeus when he met Jesus was to put his financial dealings in order and to serve the poor.

Howard will often challenge people to pray that the Lord will bring one needy person into their lives. But giving to the poor goes beyond our direct personal experience. Could you give to a church programme that helps the poor? Should you give to a Christian agency that is supporting the poor through mission and relief work?

I pray that you and I might be able to echo Job's statement: "I rescued the poor who cried for help and the fatherless who had none to assist him…I made the widow's heart sing…I was eyes to the blind and feet to the lame. I was a father to the needy; I took up the case of the stranger" (Job 29:12–16).

We have one couple that we regularly give to – they are a couple who have little, the wife is handicapped and her husband does all he can to provide for his household. On other occasions we meet a need that we see or feel called to meet. Our church, like many churches, has programmes to assist those who are most in need.

Although this area of giving can be frustrating at times, the potential benefits to the giver make it one of the most exciting and fulfilling areas in our entire Christian life.

Contrast

Society says: I would rather receive than give.

Scripture says: "It is more blessed to give than to receive" (Acts 20:35).

Commitment

Establish a time each week when you can discuss and pray about giving. Use the time to review this chapter.

thirteen
Work –
who is the real boss?

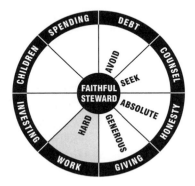

At age 29 Jonathan Thompson felt trapped. For six years he had worked as a sales assistant in a large retail store.

He was competent and the job paid moderately well. He longed, however, for a future in management, and as he looked around, he saw that all those who were promoted to management positions had university

The best way to appreciate your job is to imagine yourself without one.

Oscar Wilde

educations. So, by taking an Open University, he completed his higher education requirements and earned a degree in business administration. The company soon promoted Jonathan to a job at a much higher salary.

The first few years were just as he had imagined – reasonable hours, good salary and attractive fringe benefits. Then the unexpected happened. The company expanded to the north of England, and the Thompsons were transferred. The expansion schedule called for strict deadlines, and Jonathan assumed major responsibilities as an assistant manager. At first he enjoyed the excitement of the challenge; however, his five-day week soon became six, and his normal eight-hour day grew to 14 hours. On top of that, his new boss was so demanding that Jonathan began to experience a great deal of tension at work.

He now had more work and more responsibility, but as an assistant manager he could no longer could earn overtime. As a result, he earned the same salary as he could have received before the promotion, and resentment toward his employer was building. Jonathan began to wonder if management was worth the stress.

Jonathan's job frustrations are not unusual. Few people are completely satisfied with their jobs. Boredom, lack of fulfilment, fear of losing a job, inadequate wages, overwork and countless other pressures contribute to a high level of discontentment. Doctors, stay at home mums, dads, secretaries, salespeople, blue-collar workers and managers – regardless of the profession – the frustrations are similar.

During a 40-year career the average person spends between 60,000 and 70,000 hours working. Most of an adult's life is involved with work. Unfortunately, many just endure their work while ignoring the fact that 25 percent of their lives is devoted to a distasteful job. On the other hand, some people work too much and neglect the other priorities of life.

People usually lean to one of two extremes: they either work as little as possible because work is unpleasant, or they tend to work all the time because it becomes overwhelmingly important. Scripture affirms the value of work but teaches that we should have a balance in work. Work is designed to develop our character. While enabling us to provide for our material well-being, work is a pathway to experiencing a more intimate relationship with the Lord and with other people. In order to find satisfaction and balance in our work, we need to understand what Scripture teaches about it.

Biblical perspective of work

Even before the Fall when sin entered the human race, God instituted work. "The Lord God took the man and put him in the Garden of Eden to work it and take care of it" (Genesis 2:15). The very first thing the Lord did with Adam was to assign him work. Despite what many have come to think, work was initiated for our benefit in the sinless environment of the Garden of Eden. After the Fall, work was made more difficult. "Cursed is the ground because of you; through painful toil you will eat of it all the days of your life. It will produce thorns and thistles for you, and you will eat the plants of the field. By the sweat of your brow you will eat your food" (Genesis 3:17–19).

Work is so important that in Exodus 34:21 God gives this command: "Six days you shall labour, but on the seventh day you shall rest." The Old Testament believer was required to work six days. In the New Testament Paul is just as direct when he says "if a man will not work, he shall not eat" (2 Thessalonians 3:10). Examine the verse carefully. It says "if anyone *will not* work…" It did not say, "If anyone *cannot* work…." This principle does not apply to those who are mentally or physically unable to work. It is for those who are able but choose not to work.

A primary purpose of work is to develop character. While the builder is building a house, the house is also building the builder. Skill, diligence, manual dexterity and judgement are refined. A job is not merely a task designed to earn money; it is also intended to produce godly character in the life of the worker.

Diligence is the mother of good fortune.

Cervantes

A close friend has a sister who has been supported by her parents for more than 30 years. She has never had to face the responsibilities and hardships involved with a job. As a consequence, her character has not been properly developed and she is immature in many areas of her life.

Honourable trades and professions

Scripture does not elevate any trade or profession above another. There is dignity in all types of work, and a wide variety of vocations are represented in the Bible.

David was a shepherd and a king. Luke was a doctor. Lydia was a retailer who sold purple fabric. Daniel was a government worker. Paul was a tentmaker. Amos was a fig-picker. If God can use a fig picker, He can certainly use us in our jobs. In fact, the Saviour of the world was a carpenter. In God's economy there is equal dignity in the labour of a car mechanic and a chairman of a bank, in the labour of a senior pastor and a secretary serving the church.

God's part in work

Scripture reveals three specific responsibilities the Lord has in connection with work.

1. God gives job skills

Exodus 36:1–2 illustrates this truth: "And every skilled person to whom the Lord has given skill and ability to know how to carry out all the work" (NKJV). God has given each of us unique skills. People have widely varied abilities, manual skills and intellectual capacities. It is not a matter of one person being better than another; it is simply a matter of having received different capabilities.

2. God gives success

The life of Joseph is a perfect example. "The Lord was with Joseph and he prospered…his master saw that the Lord was with him and that the Lord gave him success in everything he did" (Genesis 39:2–3). As we have seen, you and I have certain responsibilities, but we need to recognise that it is ultimately God who gives success.

3. God seeks to direct our paths

In Proverbs 3: 5-6 we learn that if we put God first and "trust in the Lord with all your heart and lean not on your own understanding. In all your ways acknowledge Him and He will make your paths straight." One author wrote a book called 'Thank God it's Monday' which is all about bringing God into the workplace. Ultimately matters such as career development, promotion, remuneration are not just about us and our desires but about seeking God's path for our work. Many people leave God out of their work, believing that they alone are responsible for their abilities and successes. One of the major reasons they experience stress and frustration in their jobs is because they don't understand God's part in their work. Consider for a few minutes; if God gives you your abilities and has a purpose for your life including every aspect of your working life, how should this perspective affect your work?

Our part in work

All of us have certain responsibilities related to our work. Scripture reveals we are actually serving the Lord in our work and not people. "And whatever you do, do it heartily, as to the Lord and not to men, knowing that from the Lord you will receive the reward of the inheritance; for you serve the Lord Christ" (Colossians 3:23–24, NKJV). This perspective has profound implications. Consider your attitude toward work. If you could see the person of Jesus Christ as your boss, would you try to be more faithful in your job? If Jesus Christ worked for you how would you treat him, speak to him, would you expect from him just as you do your employees now? "I tell you the truth, whatever you did not do for one of the least of these, you did not do for me" (Matthew 25:45). The most important question you need to answer every day as you begin your work is: for whom do I work? You work for Christ.

Work hard

"Whatever your hand finds to do, do *it* with your might" (Ecclesiastes 9:10, NKJV). "But diligence *is* man's precious possession" (Proverbs 12:27, NKJV). In Scripture hard work and diligence are encouraged while laziness is repeatedly condemned: "One who is slack in his work is brother to one who destroys" (Proverbs 18:9). Paul's life was an example of hard work. "We worked night and day, labouring and toiling so that we would not be a burden to any of you...in order to make ourselves a model for you to follow" (2 Thessalonians 3:8–9). Your work should be at such a level that people will never equate laziness and mediocrity with God.

> *Whatever you do, do it heartily, as to the Lord and not to men.*
>
> **Colossians 3:23 NKJV**

But do not overwork! Working *too* hard has reached epidemic proportions especially for those who own their own businesses whose hours often do not meet such legislation as the Working Time Directive. A frantic, breathless, over commitment to work pervades our culture. Hard work must be balanced with the other priorities of life. Clearly our first priority is our relationship with the Lord. "But seek first His Kingdom and His righteousness" (Matthew 6:33). The second priority is the family.

If your job demands so much of your time and energy that you neglect your relationship with Christ or your family, then you are working too hard; perhaps the job is too demanding or your work habits need changing. If you tend to be a 'workaholic,' take extra precautions to guard against forsaking your other priorities.

Exodus 34:21 reads, "Six days you shall labour, but on the seventh day you shall rest; even during the ploughing season and harvest you must rest." I believe this Old Testament principle of resting one day out of seven has application for us today. This has been difficult for me, particularly when I am working under the pressure of a project deadline or financial pressure.

Rest can become an issue of faith. Is the Lord able to make our six days of work more productive than seven days? Yes! The Lord instituted this weekly rest for our physical, mental and spiritual health. The diagram below illustrates the balance God wants in our lives.

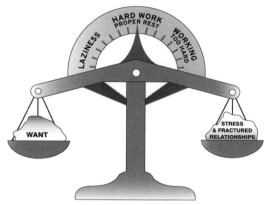

A balanced life with contentment

Employer responsibilities

The godly employer must perform a balancing act. The employer is to care for, serve and encourage the employee, but he or she must also provide leadership and hold employees accountable for their assigned tasks. Let's examine several principles that should govern an employer's conduct.

Serve your employees

The basis for biblical leadership is servant hood: "whoever wants to become great among you must be your servant" (Matthew 20:26). Too often employers have concentrated on producing a profit at the expense of their personnel. However, the Bible directs the employer to balance profit-making efforts with an unselfish concern for employees. Employees are to be treated fairly and with genuine dignity. "Masters (employers), provide your slaves with what is right and fair, because you know that you also have a Master in heaven" (Colossians 4:1).

Employers should seek creative ways to serve their employees. For example, they should consider investing time and money to educate and upgrade their employees' job skills. As employees become more capable, both employees and business can earn more.

Be a good communicator

The biblical account of building the Tower of Babel teaches the importance of good communication. At that time everyone spoke the same language and adopted a common goal of building the tower. The Lord makes this remarkable observation "if as one people speaking the same language they have begun to do this, then nothing they plan to do will be impossible for them" (Genesis 11:6).

Since building the tower was not what the Lord wanted, He stopped construction. And how did the Lord do this? He disrupted their ability to communicate. "Come, let us go down and confuse their language so they will not understand each other" (Genesis 11:7).

It is especially important to listen to employee complaints. "If I have denied justice to my menservants and maidservants when they had a grievance against me, what will I do when God confronts me? What will I answer when called to account?" (Job 31:13–14). A sensitive, listening ear is a tangible expression that you care about the other person. When a complaint is legitimate, the employer should take appropriate steps to solve the problem.

Hold employees accountable

The employer is responsible for letting employees know what is expected of them on the job. The employer should regularly evaluate their performances and communicate this to them. If an employee is not performing satisfactorily and is unable or unwilling to change, further training or possibly a personnel change may be necessary.

Pay your employees a fair wage promptly

Employers are warned to pay a fair wage. "(The Lord will judge) those who defraud labourers of their wages, who oppress the widows and the fatherless, and deprive aliens of justice, but do not fear me, says the Lord Almighty" (Malachi 3:5). They are also commanded to pay wages promptly when due. "You shall not oppress a hired (employee)…give *him* his wages, and not let the sun go down on it…lest he cry out against you to the Lord, and it be sin to you" (Deuteronomy 24:14–15, NKJV).

Employee responsibilities

We can identify the six major responsibilities of the godly employee by examining the well-known story of Daniel in the lions' den. In Daniel chapter six we are told that Darius, the king of Babylon, appointed 120 men to administer the government and three men, one of whom was Daniel, to supervise these administrators. When King Darius decided to promote Daniel to the job of governing the entire kingdom, Daniel's fellow employees tried to eliminate him. They first looked for an opportunity to discredit him in his job. After this failed, they persuaded King Darius to make a foolish decree. For a period of 30 days everyone in the kingdom would be required to worship the king only or suffer the punishment of death in the lions' den. Daniel was thrown to the lions because he continued to worship the living God. The Lord then rescued this godly employee by sending His angel to shut the lions' mouths.

Let's examine the attributes of a godly employee as demonstrated by Daniel.

Honesty

Daniel 6:4 tells us that Daniel's fellow employees could find no grounds for accusation against him in regard to his work. "They could find no corruption" in Daniel's work. He was absolutely honest.

Faithfulness

In Daniel 6:4, Daniel is described as 'trustworthy.' The godly employee needs to establish the goal of being faithful and excellent in work. Then he or she needs to work hard to attain that goal.

Prayerfulness

The godly employee is a person of prayer. "Now when Daniel learned that the decree had been published (commanding worship of the king alone)… he got down on his knees and prayed, giving thanks to his God, just as he had done before" (Daniel 6:10). Daniel governed the most powerful nation of his day. Few of us will ever be faced with the magnitude of his responsibilities and the time demands that must have been required. Yet this man knew the importance and priority of prayer. If you are not praying consistently, your work is suffering.

Honours the employer

"Daniel answered, 'O king, live for ever!'" (Daniel 6:21). What a remarkable response! The king, his employer, had been deceived and was forced into sentencing Daniel to the lions' den. But Daniel's reaction was to honour his boss. Think how natural it would have been to say something like, "You creep! The God who sent His angel to shut the lions' mouths is going to punish you!" Instead, he honoured his employer.

The godly employee always honours his boss. 1 Peter 2:18 reads, "Servants (employees), *be* submissive to *your* masters (employers) with all fear, not only to the good and gentle, but also to the harsh" (NKJV). One way to honour your employer is never to participate in gossip behind your employer's back – even if he or she is not an ideal person.

Honours fellow employees

People will play 'office politics' and may attempt to secure a promotion over you. They might even have you dismissed from your job. Daniel's peers tried to murder him! Despite this, no evidence exists that Daniel did anything but honour his fellow employees. Never slander a fellow employee. "Do not malign a servant to his master, lest he curse you, and you be found guilty" (Proverbs 30:10, NKJV).

The godly person should avoid office politics and manipulation to secure a promotion. Your superior *does not* control your promotion. The Lord Himself makes that decision. We can be content in our jobs by striving for faithfulness, honouring superiors, loving and encouraging our fellow employees. Christ will promote us if and when He chooses.

Verbalises his or her faith

At the appropriate time Daniel spoke of his faith in God to those around him. "The king spoke, saying to Daniel, 'Daniel, servant of the living God, has your God, whom you serve continually, been able to deliver you from the lions?'" (Daniel 6:20, NKJV).

King Darius would never have known about the living God if Daniel had not communicated his faith at appropriate moments during the normal conduct of his job. King Darius would not have been as powerfully influenced by Daniel's profession of faith in God if he had not observed how he did his work. Daniel fulfilled his responsibilities with honesty and faithfulness while honouring those around him. Because of this demonstration, coupled with Daniel's deliverance from the lions, Darius became a believer: "I issue a decree that in every part of my kingdom people must fear and reverence the God of Daniel. For he is the living God and he endures for ever; his kingdom will not be destroyed, his dominion will never end" (Daniel 6:26).

Daniel influenced his employer, one of the most powerful people in the world, to believe in the only true God. You have that same opportunity in your own God-given sphere of work. Let me say this another way. A job well done earns you the right to tell others with whom you work about the reality of Christ. As we view our work from God's perspective, dissatisfaction will turn to contentment from a job well done, and drudgery will be replaced with excitement over the prospect of introducing others to the Saviour.

Calling

Each of us has a specific calling or purpose which the Lord intends for us to fulfil in our work. Ephesians 2:10 reads "for we are God's workmanship, created in Christ Jesus to do good works, which God prepared in advance for us to do." Study this passage carefully. "We are God's workmanship." Each of us has been created uniquely and given special physical, emotional and mental characteristics and abilities. You probably have heard the expression "after the Lord made you, He threw away the mould!" It's true. You are gifted uniquely. No one in all of history – past, present or future – is like you.

The passage continues "created in Christ Jesus to do good works, which God prepared in advance for us to do." The Lord created each of us for a particular job, and He endowed us with the necessary skills, aptitudes and desires to accomplish this work. This calling may be full-time Christian service or a secular job. Often people struggle to know whether God wants them to continue in business once they have committed their lives to Christ. Many feel they are not serving the Lord in a significant way if they remain in a secular job. Nothing could be further from the truth. The key is for each person to determine God's call on his or her life.

Past experiences prepare us for our calling

God providentially allows us to experience circumstances to prepare us for our calling. You might find it difficult to believe that God was moulding you through your family, your environment, your education, your work and your relationships, especially if these were not godly influences. Nonetheless, He was preparing you even in the difficult experiences. For example, the Lord might use a painful, early death of a loved one to give someone the empathy and desire to counsel others in a similar situation.

Knowing our calling allows us to focus

Most of us struggle with too many things to do and too little time in which to do them. The good can become the enemy of the best. Once you have a clear vision of God's call on your life, it becomes much easier to evaluate opportunities and say 'no' to those who would distract you from what the Lord wants you to accomplish.

I have two close friends. One has only average ability, but because he has been singled-minded in his focus he has had an enormous impact. The other man is much more capable but has scattered his energies pursuing numerous projects with limited success. Knowing your calling helps you focus and become more productive.

Someone has said "work as unto the Lord…the pay's not always great, but the retirement benefits are out of this world!" This is true, and you will find an additional benefit – increased satisfaction of a job done to the best of your ability.

Retirement

The dictionary defines retirement as "withdrawal from service, office, or business, to give up or retreat from an active life." This goal is deeply ingrained in our culture. Many people retire at an arbitrary, predetermined age and cease all labour in the pursuit of a life filled with leisure.

Scripture gives no examples of people retiring. Only one direct reference to retirement is found in the Bible. It is in Numbers 8:24–26; the instruction there applied exclusively to the Levites, who worked in the tabernacle. As long as one is physically and mentally capable, no scriptural basis exists for retiring and becoming unproductive. The concept of putting an older but able person 'out to pasture' is unbiblical. Age is no obstacle to finishing the work the Lord has for you to accomplish. For example, Moses was 80 years old when he began his 40-year task of leading the children of Israel. Logic tells us that the type and intensity of work may change as we grow older – shifting gears to a less demanding pace and to becoming an 'elder at the gate.' During this season of life we can actively employ the experience and wisdom gained over a lifetime In the current economic climate many people may have to work longer to make up adequate pension provision. Others may be able to cease paid employment and commit time to service and ministry as God directs. I believe this should be the most rewarding and productive time of life. God has invested years in grooming us, and often we have more discretionary time.

Contemplating retirement? Grasp the opportunity to help build God's Kingdom!

Contrast

Society says: Work as little as possible because labour is distasteful; or work as much as possible because your job is all important.

Scripture says: Work as unto the Lord with excellence as your standard. Work hard, but do not overwork.

Commitment

Prayerfully evaluate your attitudes toward work and your job performance in light of what Scripture teaches. To help you discover any areas that need changing, ask yourself these questions:

1. Would I work more conscientiously if Jesus were my boss?
2. Would I be different at work if Jesus was my employee?
3. Would I think more highly of a chairman of a bank than a garage cashier?
4. How is my relationship with my employer, employees and fellow workers?
5. Am I trying to do too much?
6. Do my family or friendships suffer because I overwork?
7. Am I performing my job at a level of excellence?
8. Am I lazy? Do I work hard?

fourteen
Investing – steady plodding

One problem Jonathan and Helen wanted to discuss was their inability to save. "We've never been able to save consistently," Helen admitted dejectedly. "We realise this has been a mistake, and we've suffered for it.

Steady plodding
brings prosperity;
hasty speculation
brings poverty.

Proverbs 21:5, TLB

Every time the car broke down or something else went wrong, we ended up going further in debt because we didn't have savings to pay for these unexpected expenses. What should we do?"

Jonathan added "and how can we begin to invest to help provide for future needs such as our children's education and our retirement? Our children are now all young adults and are finding it almost impossible to enter the housing market. We have some friends who plan to help their children through 'equity release,' but that doesn't sit comfortably with us in view of our own financial situation."

Unfortunately, like the Thompsons most people are not regular savers. According to one source, the average person in our country is only two pay days away from bankruptcy. He or she has little or no money saved: and has significant monthly credit obligations and a total dependence on next week's / month's income to keep the budget afloat.

Saving – the Joseph principle

The Bible tells us it's wise to save. "In the house of the wise are stores of choice food and oil, but a foolish man devours all he has" (Proverbs 21:20). Because of their instinct for saving, ants are commended for their wisdom: "Four things on earth are small, yet they are extremely wise: Ants are creatures of little strength, yet they store up their food in the summer" (Proverbs 30:24–25). They put aside and save from the summer's plenty to meet a future need. Saving is the opposite of being in debt. Saving is making *provision for* tomorrow, while debt is *presumption upon* tomorrow.

Another example is Joseph, who saved during the seven years of plenty to ensure that there would be enough food during seven years of famine. I call saving the 'Joseph Principle.' Saving means to forego an expenditure today so you will have something to spend in the future. Perhaps this is why most people never save; it requires a denial of something that you want today, and our culture is not a culture of denial. When we want something, we want it *now*.

In building my three businesses I adopted the policy of giving myself the lowest level of income on which we could live. One of my directors accused me of saving like a squirrel, and it was an accusation that always resonated as having some measure of truth. When I sold the company I was retained as managing director and found that my market salary was considered enough to give me a 300% pay increase. I had retained profit in the company so that I could invest in the business deposit account so that when the business was sold I was able to extract those savings from the sale proceeds.

How to save

When you receive income, the first payment you should make is a gift to the Lord and the second payment to your savings. The Bible does not teach an amount or percentage to be saved. We recommend establishing a goal of saving at least 10 percent of your income. For many this is not possible initially, but begin the habit of saving – even it is only a pound a month.

To develop this habit you can use several different methods. For example, some commit income from bonuses to savings. Others set aside a certain percent of their regular income each month in a savings account, such as an Individual Savings Account (ISA). Still others use an automatic savings plan or an employee payroll plan. Here is a maxim for saving: if you save a portion of your income as soon as you receive it, you will save more. There are two types of savings: short-term and long-term.

Short-term savings

Short-term savings should be readily accessible. They may include interest-earning accounts. These are designed to be used for planned future spending – acquiring or replacing items such as domestic appliances and cars and making home repairs. Short-term savings should also be set aside for emergencies – an illness, loss of job, or other interruption of income. Financial advisers recommend you establish the goal of saving the equivalent of three to six months of your income for this emergency fund.

Long-term savings

Long-term savings are intended to fund long-term needs and goals such as retirement income and inheritances. Pensions and retirement accounts fall into this category. Except for extreme financial emergencies, these savings should not be used for any purpose other than the needs for which they were established.

Investing

People place some of their savings in investments with the expectation of receiving income or a growth in value. The purpose and intention of this book is *not* to recommend any specific investments. Our objective is simply to draw your attention to the following scriptural framework for investing.

The wise man saves for the future, but the foolish man spends whatever he gets.

Proverbs 21:20, TLB

Be a steady plodder

"Steady plodding brings prosperity; hasty speculation brings poverty" (Proverbs 21:5, TLB). The original Hebrew word for 'steady plodding' pictures a person filling a large barrel, one handful at a time. Little by little the barrel is filled to overflowing.

The fundamental principle you need to practice to become a successful investor is to spend less than you earn. Then save and invest the difference over a long period of time.

Examine those various investments that are well suited for "steady plodding." Your home mortgage is paid off after years of steady payments. A stock portfolio is built as it is added to each month, and a business can increase steadily in value through the years as its potential is developed.

The power of compound interest

I have always regarded this as the bedrock of an investment strategy. Save consistently, and maximise the advantage of compound interest. Sometimes referred to as the eighth wonder of the world, regular saving combined with compound interest provides a return that varies based on the amount you save, the interest rate you earn on your savings, your tax position and the length of time you save.

1. The amount. The amount you save will be determined by your level of income, the cost of your standard of living, how much debt you have, your commitment to save and how faithfully you budget. It is our hope that you will be able to increase the amount available for saving as you implement these biblical principles.

2. The interest rate. The second variable is the rate of interest you earn on an investment. The following table demonstrates how an investment of £1,000 grows at various average rates of return.

As you can see, the increase in the rate of return has a remarkable impact on the amount accumulated. A two percent increase more than doubles the amount over 40 years. However, be wary of risky investments that promise a high return. Usually the higher the rate, the higher the risk. That risk might include fluctuating interest rates. Savings institutions have a tendency to change the terms of accounts and so this type of investment, simple as it is, will require a measure of monitoring.

Interest	Year 5	Year 10	Year 20	Year 30	Year 40
4%	1,221	1,491	2,223	3,313	4,940
6%	1,348	1,819	3,310	6,023	10,957
8%	1,490	2,219	4,927	10,935	24,273
10%	1,645	2,707	7,328	19,837	53,700

The previous table does not take into account the effect of inflation. If inflation were on average three percent throughout the period the returns, expressed in today's pounds, would look like this:

Interest	Year 5	Year 10	Year 20	Year 30	Year 40
4%	1,053	1,109	1,230	1,365	1,514
6%	1,164	1,353	1,832	2,481	3,359
8%	1,285	1,652	2,728	4,505	7,441
10%	1,419	2,014	4,057	8,172	16,462

3. Time. Time is a factor we cannot control, but the graph that follows may help you visualise the benefits of starting now. If a person faithfully saves £2.74 each day – £1,000 per year – and earns 8 percent on the savings, at the end of 40 years the savings will grow to almost £290,000 and will be earning £1,207 each month in interest alone! Steady plodding pays. However, if the person waits one year before starting, then saves for 39 years, he or she will accumulate £23,000 less. The message of the illustration is this: Start saving now!

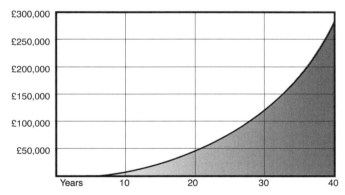

£1,000 invested each year earning 8%

Avoid risky investments

There is another serious problem I (Solomon) have seen everywhere – savings are put into risky investments that turn sour, and soon there is nothing left to pass

on to one's son. The man who speculates is soon back to where he began – with nothing. This, as I said, is a very serious problem, for all his hard work has been for nothing; he has been working for the wind. It is all swept away.
Ecclesiastes 5:13–16, TLB

Scripture warns of avoiding risky investments, yet each year thousands of people lose money in highly speculative and sometimes fraudulent investments. How many times have you heard of older people losing their life's savings on a get-rich-quick scheme? Sadly, it seems that Christians are particularly vulnerable to such schemes because they trust people who seem to live by the same values they have. I have known of investment scandals in churches where wolves in sheep's clothing fleeced the flock. There are three characteristics often associated with risky investments:

- The prospect of a large profit is 'practically guaranteed'
- The decision to invest must be made quickly. There will be no opportunity to thoroughly investigate the investment or the promoter who is selling the investment. The promoter will often be doing you a 'favour' by allowing you to invest
- Little will be said about the risks of losing money, and the investment will usually require no effort on your part

Be patient when investing. There are few who have made money in a hurry and for all those who have, the road is littered with those who have lost money, and often a significant proportion of their savings. One Christian wrote to me saying, "I am a Christian living in the UK, I live in Surrey and work in London. I was sold an investment and was never told about the risk. Now it has gone wrong and I am facing bankruptcy." Diligence, study and counsel are prerequisites for improving your likelihood for successful investments and avoiding risky ones.

Diversify

"Give portions to seven, yes to eight, for you do not know what disaster may come upon the land" (Ecclesiastes 11:2). There is no investment without risk, and Scripture does not recommend any specific investments. Money can be lost on any investment. The government can make gold illegal. Freehold property can suffer deflation. Money can be inflated until it is valueless.

The perfect investment does not exist. We need to diversify. Consider the following steps as you diversify. I recommend that you do not skip any of the steps. Start with step one, and take each step at a time.

Step 1: Save one month's living expenses and secure appropriate insurance cover.

Step 2: Save three to six months' living expenses; save for major purchases; develop your business and vocational skills. A principle in Scripture is to invest in your business or vocation, which will be productive, then build your house: "Develop your business first before building your house" (Proverbs 24:27, TLB). Many people today reverse this order. The large house, purchased too early in life, tends to require so much money that investing in business or vocation is seriously hampered.

Step 3: Purchase a home; invest conservatively to meet long term goals.

Step 4: Make other investments.

When it comes to investing, there is more to life than ISAs, stocks and shares.

Some investment options

Examples of alternative investments abound. In 1950, John Hay Whitney and his wife Betsey purchased Pablo Picasso's 'Garcon a la Pipe' (Boy with a Pipe) for $30,000. In 2004, the oil on canvas painting was sold at Sotheby's for a record-breaking $104,168,000.

However, the reality is that as with all investments, prices can go down as well as up. Alternative investments are more often than not long-term ventures, as it can take some time for them to achieve any significant increase in value. If you want to maximise the likelihood of success, you should carry out some research into your field of interest, and you should also seek qualified guidance.

Above all, when choosing alternative forms of investment, you should have a genuine interest in the field you have chosen – not only will your judgement become more informed, but you will gain real enjoyment from the process of buying and selling. It is again important to take advice before considering any such investment.

Examples of alternative investments include: art, stamps, coins, antiques, books, sports memorabilia, comics, ceramics, toys, woodlands and jewellery.

Count the cost

With every investment there are costs: financial costs, time commitments and efforts required. Sometimes investments can bring emotional stress. For example, the purchase of a rental property will require time and effort to lease and maintain. In the early years of owning a rental property, if the maximum loan of, say, 80% has been borrowed, there are risks with regard to possible interest rate rises as well as periods when there is no tenant. If the tenant is irresponsible, you may have to try to collect rent from someone who does not want to pay. Talk about emotions flaring! Before you decide on any investment, carefully consider all the costs.

Now we will focus our attention on a number of issues that are important to understand from God's perspective: balancing saving with giving, investment goals, gambling and leaving an inheritance.

Giving, saving and investing

It is scripturally permissible to save and invest only when we are also giving. Jesus told a parable that illustrates the danger of saving while not giving.

The ground of a certain rich man produced a good crop. He thought to himself, 'What shall I do? I have no place to store my crops.' Then he said, 'This is what I'll do. I will tear down my barns and build bigger ones, and there I will store all my grain and my goods. And I'll say to myself, 'You have plenty of good things laid up for many years. Take life easy; eat, drink and be merry.'' But God said to him, 'You fool! This very night your life will be demanded from you. Then who will get what you have prepared for yourself?' This is how it will be with anyone who stores up things for himself but is not rich towards God...For where your treasure is, there your heart will be also.

Luke 12:16–21, 34

The key word in this parable is 'all.' Jesus called the rich man a fool because he saved *all* of his goods, laying them up for his own use. He did not balance his saving by giving generously. It is legitimate to save and invest only when we are also giving to the Lord. Why? "Where your treasure is, there your heart will be also" (Matthew 6:21).

If we concentrate solely on saving and investing, our focus and affection will gravitate there. We will be drawn inexorably to those possessions. But if we balance our saving and investing by giving generously to the Lord, we can still love Christ first with all our heart.

Investment goals

Before you develop your individual investment strategy, you should establish investment goals. I believe there are three acceptable goals for investing:

1. Providing for your family

Paul writes in 1 Timothy 5:8 "if anyone does not provide for his relatives, and especially for his immediate family, he has denied the faith and is worse than an unbeliever." This principle extends to providing for your needs in old age and leaving an inheritance to your children.

2. Becoming financially free to serve the Lord

One objective of saving is to diminish our dependence upon a salary to meet our needs. This affords us the freedom to volunteer more time to ministry should this be what the Lord wants for us. The more my savings produce, the less I am dependent upon income from my work. Some have saved enough to be free one day a week, and others are in a position to be full-time volunteers without the need to earn a salary.

3. Operate your business

My first business was in accountancy providing accounting, tax, audit and financial services advice. The business grew quickly and so did the debt as it supported the supported the growing investment requirement in working capital. The recession of the 1980s saw the underlying value in debtors and work in progress devalue; but the increasing demand for funding meant that the overdraft grew as interest rates soared. I learnt the hard way that even when you have assets to cover liabilities, no investment is without risk. If you can plan ahead then, I believe it is proper to save and accumulate enough capital to operate a business without going into substantial debt. The amount of capital will vary, depending upon the business, capital investment, and working capital requirements of the business.

Establishing a maximum amount

When a sprinter breaks the tape at the finish line, he stops running. But many people continue accumulating more and more, even though they have achieved acceptable savings goals. I believe that each of us should establish a maximum amount we are going to accumulate, and once we have 'finished this race,' we should give away the portion of our income that we were saving. This 'finish line' on accumulation protects us against the dangers of hoarding.

Unacceptable investment goals

According to Paul in 1 Timothy 6:9–11 one investment goal, the desire to become rich, is strictly prohibited. First Timothy 6:9 states, "People who want to get rich fall into temptation and a trap and into many foolish and harmful desires that plunge men into ruin and destruction." Study this carefully. *Everyone* who wants to get rich will "fall into temptation and a trap and into many foolish and harmful desires that plunge men into ruin and destruction."

The prohibition against wanting to get rich in 1 Timothy 6:9 is followed by this passage: "For the love of money is a root of all kinds of evil" (1 Timothy 6:10). In other words, when we want to get rich, Scripture tells us that we are loving money.

I never planned to become rich. My businesses enabled me to enjoy a measure of financial success, but most of the financial rewards were not spent, they were saved. What did that achieve? At the time they did offer a measure of security, but now I realise that God's plan was for me to serve Him in full time ministry and to use the assets He entrusted to us for His purposes. Do I think I have always been a faithful steward? If I knew earlier in life what I know now, then I would certainly have done better. However, I have discussed this subject with Rhoda and we conclude that even though I didn't have the understanding I do now, I have run the financial race so far fairly well. However, if asked the question, could I have given more away, then the answer is certainly 'yes'! I am not so sure that giving is as natural as it first appears. However, it is unquestionably at the heart of God's economy.

This chapter is about investing, so let us return to our subject matter! When I focus on being a faithful steward, I am Christ-centred in my thoughts and attitudes. My actions are then motivated by a pure heart. I am serving Christ and growing closer to Him.

Matthew 6:24 says "no-one can serve two masters. Either he will hate the one and love the other, or he will be devoted to the one and despise the other. You cannot serve both God and money." When we want to get rich, we are actually loving money and hating God. We are holding on to money and despising God. We are serving money, and we are therefore not serving the living God. 1 Timothy 6:10 ends by saying "some people, eager for money, have wandered from the faith and pierced themselves with many griefs."

Toward the end of our stay in Atlanta, I read in the national newspaper, USA Today, one of its snapshot surveys. The survey question of the day addressed to those earning $50,000 asked "how much do you need to earn to be comfortable?" The average answer was $75,000 – an increase of 50%. The same question was asked of those earning $100,000 and their response was $250,000, an increase of 250%. What conclusion might be drawn from this survey? Enough is never enough – the love of money is never satisfied.

One of my core beliefs when I was building the businesses was that I was not in business to make money. On one occasion I was in Chicago negotiating a publishing contract and during the discussions about price I was told quite directly by Irwin, the owner of the publishing rights, that I needed to understand that he *loved* money. That interjection jarred at the time and subsequently caused me to understand why I was in business. By this time I was building the second business and enjoying some good success. I determined that my priorities in business were firstly to meet and exceed the needs of my customers and secondly to provide a happy and challenging workplace for my employees.

I decided that the extent to which I achieved these goals would be directly reflected in profits. I believe that the purpose of a business is to meet the needs of its customers and one of the outcomes of achieving that is that the business will be successful and one of the results of being successful is that the business will make a profit. Thus one of my benchmarks was profit and not money. The difference? For me, it was all down to attitude and focus: if all you ever do is to focus on the bottom line, you will miss out on opportunities to grow the business and increase profitability.

There is nothing wrong with having wealth as this is a consequence of being a faithful steward. However, the Bible is replete with warnings against the love of money. In God's economy there is an emphasis on giving. This chapter is about steady plodding, but we cannot look at this aspect of our finances in isolation.

Split and submit

We overcome the temptation to get rich by remembering to split and submit. In 1 Timothy 6:11 Paul counsels Timothy to "flee from all this (the desire to get rich), and pursue righteousness, godliness, faith, love, endurance and gentleness." When you become aware of your desire to become rich, you must flee (split) from that temptation and replace it with the pursuit of godliness.

Next, submit. The ultimate way of escape is found in submitting to Jesus as Lord. We can do this in perfect confidence because Jesus overcame the temptation to become rich. After Christ fasted 40 days in the wilderness, the devil tempted Him three times. The final temptation is recorded in Luke 4:5–7: the devil led him up to a high place and showed him in an instant all the kingdoms of the world. The devil said to him, "I will give you all their authority and splendour,... if you worship me, it will all be yours."

Can you imagine what an incredible temptation this would present?

When Howard was in the property development business and discovered a prime piece of property, he would almost immediately begin to covet it and revel in the possibility of becoming rich. Jesus was exposed to all the kingdoms of the world in a moment of time. But because He was submitted entirely to the Father and empowered by the same Holy Spirit who lives in us, He was able to resist that temptation.

I believe that our heavenly Father will never ultimately prosper His children when they are motivated to get rich. Wanting to get rich – loving money – closely parallels greed. And "greed...which is idolatry" (Colossians 3:5). The Father watches jealously over His children to ensure that we will not be drawn away from loving Him with all our hearts.

Gambling and lotteries

Government-sanctioned lotteries and all types of online gambling (often called gaming) are sweeping our nation. A recent study shows that over £1 billion is gambled in the UK every week. There are now over 2,000 websites devoted to online gambling and advertisements offer 'free' gambling in order to promote the gambling habit. One study reported that the average church member gives £20 a year to foreign missions while the average person who gambles spends £1,200 a year!

Sadly, there are hundreds of thousands of compulsive gamblers who regularly deplete their family income. Their stories are heart-breaking. The Bible does not specifically prohibit gambling; however, many who gamble do so in an attempt to get rich quickly. This is a violation of Scripture.

As men and women who serve a holy God, we are called to be salt and light to a lost world. I firmly believe we need to make a commitment *never* to participate in gambling or lotteries even for entertainment. We should not expose ourselves to the risk of becoming compulsive gamblers, nor should we support an industry that enslaves so many.

Inheritance

Parents should attempt to leave a material inheritance for their children: "a good man leaves an inheritance for his children's children" (Proverbs 13:22). The inheritance should not be dispensed until the child has been thoroughly trained to be a wise steward "an inheritance quickly gained at the beginning will not be blessed at the end" (Proverbs 20:21).

In my opinion, you should provide for the inheritance to be distributed over several years or when the heir is mature enough to handle the responsibility of money. Some Wills do not provide for a fully accessible inheritance until the age of either 18, 21 or sometimes beyond. In these circumstances a Will often provides for the establishment of a trust with trustees appointed to help supervise the use of those funds. "What I am saying is that as long as the heir is a child, he is no different from a slave, although he owns the whole estate, but he is subject to guardians and trustees until the time set by his father" (Galatians 4:1–2).

You should provide an inheritance for your children. However, it probably is not wise to leave your children with great wealth if they have not been thoroughly schooled in the biblical perspective of money and how to properly manage it. I have counselled many wealthy individuals who were concerned about the effect their wealth would have in the hands of their children. I am sure you can think of heirs and heiresses whose behaviour might cause concern if they were your children. An inheritance can turn out to be a curse. No one has the right to handicap his children with such a burden as great wealth. He must face this question squarely: Will the fortune be safe with my child, and will my child be safe with my fortune?

Wills

The majority of people who die do not have a current Will. It is often reported that six out of seven people do not have a Will. That is a statistic that I have never found proven among the people that I counsel. However, it may well be that six out of seven people do not have a Will or one that is up-to-date – or that reflects their current circumstances and/or wishes and intentions. Think of what this means. To die without a Will is expensive and time consuming and can be heartbreaking for your loved ones. It can literally destroy an estate left to provide for the family.

Scripture teaches that we brought nothing into the world and we will take nothing with us when we die, but we *can* leave behind our money and possessions precisely as we wish. We can specify to whom and how much. If you die without a Will, these decisions become subject to intestacy law which may, and almost certainly will, result in your estate being distributed in a way that would not meet with your wishes. If you leave minor children, it will be Social Services who decide who will look after them. In that case, they may select someone who may not know the Lord. In order to encourage clients to make a Will, I used to ask them if they would like the government to decide who should look after their children. I cannot recall a client that who did not then make out their Will.

Whether you are married or single, rich or poor, you should have a Will. Not only does it clear up any legal uncertainties, it also helps you map out your finances while you are alive so that you can protect the best interests of your heirs.

About one in six of the population dies before retirement age. So do not put off preparation of your Will just because you may be young. Do it now! As Isaiah told Hezekiah "this is what the Lord says: put your house in order, because you are going to die; you will not recover" (2 Kings 20:1). Someday, should the Lord tarry, you will die. One of the greatest gifts you can leave your family for that emotional time will be an organised estate and a properly prepared Will. If you do not have a current Will, please make an appointment with a solicitor to prepare one.

Contrast

Society says: Spend all you make. However, if you should save, put your trust in your accumulated assets.

Scripture says: "The wise man saves for the future, but the foolish man spends whatever he gets" (Proverbs 21:20, TLB).

Commitment

1. Establish a pattern of saving. Start with your next pay cheque.
2. Make an appointment with a solicitor this week to have your Will prepared.

fifteen
Children –
the abc of money

Learning to handle money one step at a time is part of a child's education, a part that parents cannot leave to teachers but must oversee themselves. Spending experiences are found in the outside world rather than in the classroom.

I have made it one of my priorities to teach my children how to handle money. From an early age they were all given pocket money, an amount that was usually less than the weekly allowance given by parents to their school friends. We taught them to give and to save and helped them through how they felt when they did not have enough money to buy some of the things they would have liked. After introducing them to Jesus Christ and giving them a happy and secure home I regarded teaching them how to handle finances as one of my main missions.

Train up a child in the way he should go, and when he is old he will not depart from it.

Proverbs 22:6, KJV

In the first week of the Crown small group study we ask "what did you find most interesting or challenging when reading this book?" We are not alone in reporting that this chapter and the responsibility to train children is one that speaks to some in a penetrating manner.

The world seeks from an early age to hook our children on wants, whether it is toys or clothes and gadgets for our teens. Then, as soon as they are old enough, get ready, as through your letter box will come myriad invitations to apply for credit cards, including ones that are already 'pre-approved.' Then they're off to university and at Freshers Fare they will be inundated with offers of credit cards 'so you can charge your books and coffee to the card.' That could well make the coffee more expensive than the legendary coffee prices at the restaurants bordering San Marco Square in Venice!

Children don't always appreciate the value of money. What should you do? This is a question all parents need to answer.

In 1904 Wales experienced a remarkable revival. The effects of the revival were widespread. An estimated 100,000 converts were added to the church during the two years the revival lasted, including previously hardened unbelievers. Drunkards, thieves, gamblers were transformed. Miners prayed together before commencing their shifts in the coal-mines. Pit-ponies, unused to the new kindness and clean language – without the usual kicks and curses – almost stopped work until they got adjusted. Courts had few cases to try. Whole football and rugby teams got converted and fixtures were abandoned. Dance halls were deserted, the pubs were empty and not a few went out of business, but the prayer meetings were crowded (from Great Revivals, Colin Whitaker). Wales also sent missionaries all over the world.

One of those missionaries travelled to Argentina, where on the streets, he led a young boy to Christ. The boy's name was Luis Palau. He has since become known as the 'Billy Graham' of Latin America. Out of gratitude for this Welsh missionary, Palau travelled to Wales during the early 1970s to express his thankfulness to that nation for helping lead him to Christ. What he discovered was astonishing. Less than one half of one percent of the Welsh attended church. Divorce was at an all-time high, and the crime rate was escalating rapidly. Many churches had closed and been converted to bars, and rugby had replaced Christianity as the national religion.

As a result of this experience, Palau produced a film entitled *God Has No Grandchildren*. The thrust of the film is that each generation is responsible for passing on the faith to the next. In Wales, despite tremendous spiritual vitality, the impact of Christianity had all but disappeared in 70 years. Parents had failed to pass their faith on to their children. Each generation is responsible for passing on to its children the gospel and the truths of Scripture, including God's financial principles.

When you left home, how well prepared were you to make financial decisions? Parents and teachers spend 18 to 22 years preparing youth for occupations, but generally less than a few hours teaching children the value and use of the money they will earn during their careers. To teach biblical principles of handling money, parents should use these three methods: verbal communication, modelling and practical experience.

Verbal communication

The Lord charged the Israelites "and these words which I command you today shall be in your heart. You shall teach them diligently to your children, and shall talk of them when you sit in your house, when you walk by the way, when you lie down, and when you rise up" (Deuteronomy 6:6–7 NKJV). We must verbally instruct our children in the ways of the Lord, but children need more than mere verbal instruction; they also need a good example.

Modelling for our children

Children soak up parental attitudes toward money like a blotter soaks up ink. Parents need to be models of how to handle money faithfully. Paul recognised the importance of example when he said, "Follow my example, as I follow the example of Christ" (1 Corinthians 11:1). The Lord used both of these techniques. He gave us His written Word, the Bible, and also sent the perfect model, Jesus Christ, to demonstrate how we should live. Luke 6:40 is a challenging passage for parents. It reads "a student is not above his teacher, but everyone who is fully trained will be like his teacher." Another way of saying this is that we can teach what we believe, but we only reproduce who we are. We must be good models.

Practical experiences

Children then need to be given opportunities to apply what they have heard and seen. There are learning experiences which benefit the child in the area of money management (the art of wise spending) and money making (the value of work).

Learning experiences in 'money management'

Learning to handle money should be part of a child's education. Parents must direct this themselves and not delegate it to teachers because spending experiences are found outside the classroom. Consider five areas where this is possible:

1. Income

As soon as the child is ready for school, he or she should begin to receive an income to manage. Even a four year old enjoys having money to buy sweets! The parents need to decide whether they wish to give an allowance or require their child to earn the income. Choose the alternative with which you are most comfortable.

The amount of the income will vary according to such factors as the child's age and ability to earn. However, the amount is not as important as the responsibility of handling money. At first it is a new experience, and the child will make many mistakes. Don't hesitate to let the "law of natural consequences" run its course. You're going to be tempted to help little Connor when he spends all his income the first day on an unwise purchase. He won't like the fact that he has to live the rest of the week without all the other things he wants and maybe needs. *Don't bail him out.* His mistakes will be his best teacher.

Parents should establish boundaries and offer advice on how to spend money, but your child must have freedom of choice. Excessive restrictions will only reduce his opportunities to learn by experience. The first few pennies will make a lasting impression. Every Saturday we would give our children their pocket money. Philip, our eldest, would often spend it when out with his friends at the shops. Often his money would go on bubble gum in order to extend his collection of soccer cards. I am sure he learnt how to survey at school, he seemed to know how much pocket money everyone else was getting in the class and we were made to feel like a couple of meanies. Having built up a large pile of cards they were consigned to his drawer as he elected to budget his money so it lasted for the week.

Parents should slowly increase the income as the child grows in his or her ability and demonstrates wise spending patterns.

2. Budgeting

When children begin to receive an income, teach them how to budget. Begin with a simple system consisting of three boxes, each labelled by category – give, save and spend. The child distributes a portion of his income into each box. Thus, a simple budget is established using visual control. When the box is empty, there is no money to spend. Even a six-year-old can understand this method. You could use a shoe box and make a money box one Saturday morning. Divide the box into three compartments and on the outside label the sections with the three categories. Then complete the money box with three coin slots and remember to make sure the money cannot slide underneath from one compartment to another. If this happens the money may slide from saving to spending!

By the time a child is 15, he or she is old enough to be exposed to the family's budget. He will understand that he is growing up because he can now share in making plans for spending the family income. He will realise that each member has a responsibility for wise spending, regardless of who provides the income. As the child matures, he should participate in every aspect of the family budget. It will help him to realise the extent and limitations of the family income as well as how to make the money stretch to meet the family's needs.

At first the child may think that the family has so much money that it is impossible to spend it all. To help him visualise the budget, have the family income converted to a bag full of pound coins. Place these on a table and divide the 'income' pile into the various 'expense' piles representing the categories of spending. It is often difficult for children to grasp numbers because they are abstract. The coins will provide a tangible way for a child to understand the family budget.

During the budget training, teach your child to become a wise consumer. Teach shopping skills, the ability to distinguish needs from wants and the fine art of waiting on the Lord to provide. Warn the child about the powerful influence of advertising and the danger of impulse spending. When the child becomes a teenager, discontinue the allowance unless he presents a budget that accounts for how the last week's allowance was spent. Encourage them to use a budgeting software program.

3. Giving

The best time to establish the personal habit of giving is when you are young. It is helpful for children to give a portion of their gifts to a tangible need they can visualise. For example, a child can understand the impact of a gift when the contribution is helping to buy new equipment for the worship team or when it is buying food for a needy family they know.

Dr. Richard Halverson, former chaplain of the U.S. Senate, gave his son Chris this rich heritage as a child. Through a ministry that serves poor children, Chris and his brother gave money to support a Korean orphan named Kim who had lost his sight and an arm during the Korean War. Chris was taught to feel that Kim was his adopted brother. One Christmas, Chris bought Kim a harmonica. It was Kim's first personal possession. He cherished this gift from Chris and learned to play it well. Today Kim is an evangelist, and in his presentation of the gospel he includes playing the harmonica. By being trained to give as a youth, Chris experienced firsthand the value of meeting people's needs and seeing God change lives as a result of faithful giving.

When your child is a teenager, a family or church mission trip to a Third World country can be a powerful experience. Direct exposure to abject poverty can initiate a lifetime of giving to the poor. We also recommend a family time each week for dedicating that week's gifts to the Lord. It is important for the children to participate in this time of dedication and worship. The more involved children are with their parents in the proper handling of money, the better habits they will have as adults.

4. Saving and investing

The habit of saving should be established as soon as the child receives an income. It is helpful to open a savings account for your child at this time. As the child matures, you also should expose him or her to various types of investments – interest savings accounts, unit trusts, stocks and shares and of course the ISA 'savings wrapper.'

You may also have a child trust fund which your child can access from the age of 18. How much is invested? How might they wish to use this investment? Share with them who has added to this investment, so they may have the opportunity to say 'thank you.'

Teach your children the benefits of compounding interest. If they grasp this concept and become faithful savers, they will enjoy financial stability as adults. Parents should demonstrate saving by doing so for something that will directly affect and benefit the children. A good example is a family holiday. Use a graph the children can fill in so they can chart the progress of the family's saving.

Children should have both short-term and long-term saving programmes. The younger the child, the more important are short-term achievable goals. To a four-year-old, a week seems like a lifetime to save for a small purchase. He or she will not understand about saving for future education or retirement but will get excited about saving for a small toy. Long-term saving for education, the first car, etc. should be a requirement. Some parents find it motivating to their child if they add an amount equal to their child's contribution to their long-term savings.

5.Debt

It is also important to teach the cost of money and how difficult it is to get out of debt. Jim Snaith loaned his son and daughter the money to buy bicycles. Jim drew up a loan agreement with a schedule for repayment of the loan. He included the interest charged. After they successfully went through the long, difficult process of paying off the loan, the family celebrated with a 'loan burning' ceremony. Jim said that his children have appreciated those bikes more than any of their other possessions, and they have vowed to avoid debt in the future.

Learning experiences in 'money making'

Because work is an essential element in becoming a faithful steward, parents have the responsibility to train each child in the value of work and proper work habits. If a child responds and learns how to work with a proper attitude, then he or she will not only have taken a giant step to becoming content, but he or she will become a valuable asset in the job market. Good employees are difficult to find. Clearly, children need to learn the dignity and habit of work. There are four areas to consider in this training:

1. Establish routine responsibilities

The best way for a child to become faithful in work is to establish the habit of daily household chores. For example, my son carries out the bin and loads the dishwasher. And when our daughter lived at home she used to help with the household cleaning and shopping.

2. Expose your children to your work

Many young children wish to increase their income and cannot wait until they are legally old enough to do a part-time job, such as delivering newspapers. Some give part of their income to help the family budget. You might not need the money to balance the books, but here is an opportunity to allow them to share in the costs of running the home – even if they only give a token amount. In doing so they will readily learn responsibility and the value of money. There is also an opportunity to share and learn how their parent(s) earn(s) the family income.

During a Crown class, one participant said that he asked his father what he did at work. "I make money," the father replied. "For a long time I thought my dad actually made pound coins," he said.

Four children were talking together about how their parents got money. Here is what they said:

"My mum asked my dad 'how much did you draw this week?' I thought he was a great artist to be able to do all that detailed lettering and artwork."

"Well, I didn't ask my mum where the money comes from because I know. Every time mum and I go to the supermarket the person at the till asks my mum if she would like some cash."

"I sometimes go with my dad to the hole in the wall and he takes as much money as we need. Seems funny to me getting money out of a rock!"

"My mum and dad just use plastic – they have a lot of it as well"

For these children this was their reality – let yours know the role work plays in how you earn your money.

An important way to teach the value of work is to expose the child to the parents' means of earning a living. If your children cannot visit you at work, at least take the time to explain your job to them. For those parents who manage their own businesses, allow your children to participate when they are legally able to do so. Our children have all spent some time working in the businesses. Our eldest, Philip, has worked for almost ten years in one of the businesses we once owned.

One word of advice, because many children do not see their parents at work, the parents' work attitudes and habits around the home will be a major modelling influence. If a parent works hard at the factory or office but complains about washing the dishes at home, what's being communicated to the children about work? Examine your work attitudes and activities at home to ensure that you are properly influencing your children to be godly workers.

3. Earn extra money at home

Encourage your child to do extra work to earn money. A good rule of thumb is to pay the child a fair wage for the work you would have to hire someone to do. For example, if your car needs washing and your daughter needs some extra money and wants to wash it, let her. Be happy to pay her rather than the car wash.

4. Encourage your child to work for others

When they are old enough, a paper round, baby-sitting job, shop assistant work or waiter/waitress job will serve as an education. A job gives a child an opportunity to enter into an employee-employer relationship and to earn extra money.

As your child enters senior school it maybe a good idea to discontinue allowances during the summer holidays. This will motivate them to earn their own money by taking a summer job. Moreover, some students can handle part-time work during the school year.

The objective of training your child in the value of work is to build and discipline character. A working child with the proper attitude will be a more satisfied individual. He or she will grow up with more respect for the value of money and what is required to earn it.

Dependence, danger and destruction

Fathers in our country spend less time with their children than fathers in almost every other nation of the world. Many fathers currently spend less than fifteen minutes per day communicating with their sons. King David and Eli, the priest, were both godly men who had remarkably productive careers. Yet both lost sons through careless fathering.

If children are going to thrive, it will be because parents place them high on their list of priorities, consistently reserving an adequate portion of their time and energy for leadership within their homes. Fathers, I encourage you to seize the opportunity to train your children. You can literally influence generations. It is very common these days for a single mother to be the head of the household. I appreciate the demands these mothers face. But please be encouraged. Some of the most responsible children I have ever met have been raised by godly mothers alone.

I know one single mum who has five daughters; they are such mature responsible children who do all they can to help. The household budget would not balance without their commitment to part-time work.

Dependence on prayer

One of the most valuable lessons you can teach your children is to pray for the Lord's guidance and provision. The Lord wants to demonstrate that He is actively involved in each of our lives. One way He does this is by answering our prayers. Because of our affluent society, we often rob ourselves of this opportunity. We can buy things or charge purchases to 'plastic' without prayerfully allowing the Lord to supply them. We need to be creative in how we can experience the reality of God in the area of our spending, and we need to be careful to communicate that value to our children. Praying about whether we should buy something is a good way of extending out faith into our finances. Encourage children to pray about their spending decisions.

Danger of television

Television has affected children in ways we have not yet begun to fathom. Consider these statistics: by the time the typical teenager leaves school, he has spent 12,960 hours in class and 13,250 hours in front of the TV. Children spend more time watching television than any other activity except sleeping and study. Most of the damage does not come from programmes or advertisements that directly attack biblical standards, but from those that make anti-scriptural assumptions and whose attack is subtle and indirect. The influence of television on children is so pervasive and potentially dangerous that parents cannot afford to ignore it. Rather, they must restrict and regulate television if they are to be successful in training their children to be faithful stewards.

Danger of the Internet

Playing games, researching, checking the latest sport updates, shopping for a last minute bargain, socialising and Internet banking are just some examples of why the Internet is considered so important. While I agree with this statement I could easily ask myself "what would I do without the Internet?" I must put into perspective that there can be a negative flip side, especially where children are concerned.

We often hear of news reports of children meeting up with strangers online, and with chat rooms and social networking sites such as *Facebook* and *Myspace*. Parents should either ban, or create an age limit when their child can access these sites, explaining their reasons for their actions. Routine checking is advisable. If you have a family shared computer, create user names for each child, with security locks for parental control so you can check their Internet viewing history.

Time and money are easily wasted. Internet spending is increasing rapidly, due to its increased popularity both for business and for home. While auction sites can be useful to find a bargain they can easily entice inexperienced users, such as children, with their cheap retail prices but often expensive delivery costs. Again it's a good idea to keep check, asking questions if necessary.

Some sites are unsuitable for children; these include 'adult sites' and online gambling (gaming). These can be accidentally accessed as well, with popup windows randomly appearing on screen. It is therefore advisable to have an Internet blocker or firewall protection to prevent this from happening. These blockers can also prevent popup windows and adverts that can easily entice children into unwanted scams.

Destruction of over indulgence

When it comes to money, parents are often on a tightrope trying to keep a proper balance. They can easily be too miserly with money. In our affluent culture, however, they are more often over indulgent, and consequently can hamper the development of their child's character. How many of us know of a father who once sold newspapers to earn a bicycle and now has a teenage son who drives a sports car? Clearly, over indulgence with money can retard the development of a child's character and destroy the need for initiative and motivation. Too often it creates in a child a constant expectation to be given things without having to work or save for them.

Strategy for independence

Finally, we need to establish a strategy for independence. Work toward having each child independently managing all of his or her own finances (with the exception of food and shelter) by the time they are fifteen. In this way you are available to advise the children as they learn to make spending decisions.

Let's review the three steps for training children:

1. Verbally communicate biblical principles of handling money. Crown Financial Ministries has developed a series of three studies for children – one for teens, one for children ages 8 to 12, and a study for children under 8. Parents can use these very effectively to train their children.

2. Become models of financial faithfulness, allowing your children to observe closely how you apply these principles.

3. Create practical opportunities for your children to experience God's financial principles. Each child has an individual personality and temperament. One child may spend wildly yet be very generous; another may save everything and never want to give. You need to study your children's personalities carefully and tailor the training to fit the child.

As Wales discovered, God has no grandchildren. Passing on our faith in Christ to the next generation can be compared to a relay race. Any track coach will tell you that relay races are often won or lost in the passing of the baton from one runner to another. As an avid watcher of the 4x100 metre races at the Olympics, we have far too often seen a medal position slip through the fingers – just like the baton.

As parents we have the responsibility to pass the baton of practical biblical truths to our children. At times during the training it may seem as if there is little progress. Nonetheless, be consistent and persistent!

I know few adults whose parents lived all of these biblical financial principles and taught them systematically to their children. As an unfortunate consequence of this lack of training, children have left home ill-equipped to manage their financial future according to Scripture. I pray our generation will leave our children the blessed legacy of financial faithfulness.

Contrast

Society says: They will work it out as they go along.

Scripture says: Parents have the obligation to train a child to be a faithful steward and a wise money manager.

Commitment

Evaluate what your children are learning about work and handling money. Consider using the Crown Financial Ministries children's studies to train them to become faithful stewards.

sixteen
Budget –
keep abreast of the facts

The day Rhoda and I went to see Helen Thompson's parents, David and Mary Webster, they were enjoying the visit of their youngest granddaughter, Heather. As they watched her play, there was not even a hint of what they had gone through the previous year. For the Websters it had been a year of dramatic upheaval. David had suffered a stroke that paralysed his left side and caused him to lose his job. They were forced to sell their cosy detached four bedroom home and readjust to a much lower standard of living.

Annual income twenty pounds, annual expenditure nineteen six, result happiness. Annual income twenty pounds, annual expenditure twenty pounds ought and six, result misery.

Charles Dickens

The clean, neat apartment they now called home was sparsely furnished. It was apparent that they were going through hard times. Mary explained their readjustment. "We have been amazed at what we can live without. We have been forced to watch every penny and follow a strict budget."

Their backs were against a financial wall, and the Websters had responded by economising at every turn. They went without their car, no longer ate out at restaurants and limited the use of the hot water heater to

30 minutes a day – just enough for showers and the dishes. Their conservation was paying off. They were actually putting more money into savings than when they were living on David's lucrative salary as an engineer. However, during those years of easy spending, they had lived without the restraints of a budget. "The trauma of unemployment forced us to communicate in an area of our lives that had been 'off limits' during the 'good old days,'" Mary explained. "We have learned more about each other through this adversity than at any other time during our 37 years of marriage. As strange as this may sound, we are grateful that this hardship happened. There is more peace in our family now than during the years of prosperity."

What is a budget?

The Websters are proof that when we plan where our money is to go, we can make the money go further. That's what a budget is – a plan for spending money.

Why budget?

When the bank notified the customer of his overdraft he replied in disbelief "I must have more money left in my account. I still have six cheques in my cheque book!" Like the surprised customer, if you do not have a written budget, chances are that you are flying by the seat of your financial pants.

Budgeting does not automatically come to mind as the ideal way to spend free time, but it is the only way to follow through and apply what has been learned about getting out of debt, saving and giving while still meeting basic personal and household needs. Balancing income and expenditure and either staying out of debt or getting out of debt comprise some of the essentials of good housekeeping. Budgeting allows you to plan the priorities of the fixed household costs, giving and saving and other needs and expenditures. Regardless of income, many have difficulty making ends meet unless there is a plan for spending. Costs always seem to rise just a little more than income. I have seen many examples of this. Regardless of what a person earns, he or she may well struggle toward the end of the week or month unless there is a spending plan in place that is accompanied by a disciplined approach to spending. Using a budget introduces an attitude of control in spending that is needed to reach financial objectives.

Budgeting provides an opportunity to pray about spending decisions

This is important because according to one survey, more than 70 percent of marital breakdowns cite financial mismanagement as one of the causes. I seldom see a family with financial problems where there is not real tension within the marriage.

A successful budget should be a joint effort. It is a good communication tool for the husband and wife to use. A budget also can help a family get full value for its money without losing sight of the things family members want most.

A family in our church is committed to sending their children to youth camp each summer for a week. Several years ago as they were planning their annual budget in January, it became apparent that there would not be enough money for the children to go to youth camp. The family then agreed everyone would 'contribute' to camp by making a sacrifice: the father gave up his monthly game of golf, the mother did not join her tennis club and the children received half their normal pocket money. By using a budget, the family was able to anticipate a problem and adjust their spending to enable them to get what they wanted most, in this case youth camp.

How to budget

A budget is useful only if it is used. It should be a plan specifically tailored for managing *your* finances, not someone else's. Some people are more comfortable using a hand-written system, while others prefer using a budget system on a spreadsheet.

To prepare your budget follow these three steps:

Step one – start where you are now

Developing a budget must begin with your current situation. Determine exactly how much household income and expenditure you have. Some people do not know what they are actually earning and spending. For this reason it is essential to keep a record of every penny for a week/month to gain an accurate picture in order to complete an estimated budget.

If your wages or salary are not the same each month (like the income of a commissioned salesperson), make a conservative estimate of your annual income and divide by 12 to establish a working figure for your monthly income.

Then determine which expenses do not necessarily occur each month. Examples are water and gas/electricity, holidays, birthdays and Christmas. Estimate how much these cost for a year and divide that amount by 12 to determine your monthly cost. If you have not kept your bills or receipts, check with your bank and/or credit statement records to see how much you paid. Armed with this information, you can complete the Estimated Weekly/Monthly Budget on the next pages. Do not be discouraged. Almost every budget starts out with expenditure in excess of income. But a solution exists.

Step two – the solution is where we want to be

To solve the problem of spending more than your income, you must either increase your income or decrease your expenditures. It is that simple: you need to either earn more or spend less.

Increasing your income

A part-time job, or possibly a project that would involve others in the family are ways of increasing your income. The ever-present danger of increasing income is the tendency for expenses also to rise. To avoid this problem agree to apply any additional income to balancing the budget. Another potential concern is the effect that dedicating more time to work will have on relationships, both within the family and outside in order to earn more money. The 'pain' in order to make the 'gain' needs to be considered.

Reducing your expenditure

I had many clients who were in seasonal businesses. Some owned holiday lets, others in the fishing tackle and garden centre trades. Whenever I was involved with cash flow planning for seasonal businesses we would always

Estimated weekly budget

Gross income

Gross income: _____

Salary _____
Benefits _____
Dividends _____
Other income _____

Deduct:
1. Giving: _____
2. Taxes: _____
3. Other deduction: _____ _____

Net Spendable Income A: £ _____

Living expenses

3. Housing: _____

Mortgage/rent _____
Insurance _____
Council tax _____
Electricity _____
Gas _____
Water/sewage _____
Telephone _____
Maintenance _____
Garden supplies _____
Other _____

4. Food/supermarket: _____

5. Transport: _____

Payments _____
Fuel _____
Insurance _____
Vehicle duty _____
Repair replacement _____
Other: _____

6. Insurance: _____

Life _____
Sickness _____
Other _____

7. Debts: _____

(except car and
mortgage payments)

8. Entertainment/recreation: _____

Babysitters _____
Holidays _____
Pets _____
Other _____

9. Clothing: _____

10. Savings: _____

11. Medical costs: _____

Dentist _____
Prescriptions _____
Other _____

12. Miscellaneous*: _____

Toiletries/cosmetics* _____
Laundry/cleaning _____
Allowances _____
Subscriptions _____
Birthdays/anniv. _____
Events _____
Christmas presents _____
Postage _____
Professional/legal _____
Other _____

13. School/Child Care: _____

Tuition _____
Day care _____
Other _____

14. Investments: _____

Total living expenses £_____

Income vs. Living Costs

Net Spendable Income: **A**_____

Deduct: Total living expenses: **B**_____

Surplus or Deficit: £_____

*Where not included in the supermarket account

Estimated monthly budget

Gross income

Gross income: _____

  Salary _____

  Benefits _____

  Dividends _____

  Other income _____

Deduct:

1. Giving: _____

2. Taxes: _____

3. Other deduction: _____ _____

Net Spendable Income A: £ _____

Living expenses

3. Housing: _____

  Mortgage/rent _____

  Insurance _____

  Council tax _____

  Electricity _____

  Gas _____

  Water/sewage _____

  Telephone _____

  Maintenance _____

  Garden supplies _____

  Other _____

4. Food/supermarket: _____

5. Transport: _____

  Payments _____

  Fuel _____

  Insurance _____

  Vehicle duty _____

  Repair replacement _____

  Other: _____

6. Insurance: _____

  Life _____

  Sickness _____

  Other _____

7. Debts: _____

(except car and
mortgage payments)

8. Entertainment/recreation: _____

  Babysitters _____

  Holidays _____

  Pets _____

  Other _____

9. Clothing: _____

10. Savings: _____

11. Medical costs: _____

  Dentist _____

  Prescriptions _____

  Other _____

12. Miscellaneous*: _____

  Toiletries/cosmetics* _____

  Laundry/cleaning _____

  Allowances _____

  Subscriptions _____

  Birthdays/anniv. _____

  Events _____

  Christmas presents _____

  Postage _____

  Professional/legal _____

  Other _____

13. School/Child Care: _____

  Tuition _____

  Day care _____

  Other _____

14. Investments: _____

Total living expenses £_____

Income vs. Living Costs

Net Spendable Income: **A** _____

Deduct: Total living expenses: **B** _____

Surplus or Deficit: **£** _____

*Where not included in the supermarket account

look at the ability of the business to pay an even amount of income to the owner throughout the year. There was no point in taking high income during the busy times only to find there was no spare cash when the prime season had past. I also had actor clients and many of them would have other employment in between their acting engagements.

Similarly, if you have fluctuating income, maybe because of commissions, or because you are self-employed, prepare your budget taking a pessimistic viewpoint of your income. Which items of expenditure are absolutely necessary? Which can I do without? Which can I reduce?

You can ask these same questions of your personal budget as you reduce spending. Here are some suggestions to help you evaluate your major expenses.

In order to take a preliminary view of your budget, the crownuk.org website has a range of household costs which look at the key components that comprise the average family budget.

Accommodation

1. Purchase an older house that you can improve with yourself. You can also buy a smaller house suitable to your needs today with a design that can be expanded to meet your future needs.
2. Consider apartment living. It can be less expensive and involves fewer responsibilities – garden care, maintenance, etc.
3. If you can do repair and maintenance work such as garden care, maintenance, painting and carpet cleaning, you will save a substantial amount.
4. Shop carefully for furniture and household appliances. Car boot sales are a good source of reasonably priced household goods.
5. Which appliances could be switched off? Double glazing and roof insulation reduce energy consumption. Good housekeeping can save 15% of your energy supplies so make sure you don't leave appliances on. Even if you leave the plug in the socket, this uses up energy!
6. Lower the cost of your energy supplies by limiting the use of heating, lights and appliances. Use energy saving light bulbs and A-rated appliances. See energysavingtrust.org.uk for more details.

Food

1. Avoid throwing food away because it has 'gone off' or is out-of-date.

2. Prepare a menu for the week. Then list the ingredients from the menu and shop according to the list. This will help you plan a nutritionally balanced diet, avoid impulse shopping and eliminate waste.

3. Shop once a week. Each time we go shopping for "some little thing," we always seem to buy "some other little thing" as well.

4. Reduce the ready to eat meals, which have expensive packing added to the cost.

5. Leave children and hungry spouses at home when shopping. The fewer distractions the better.

6. Lunches eaten out are often budget breakers. A lunch prepared at home and taken to work will help the budget and the waistline.

7. Reduce the use of disposable products. Paper plates, cups and napkins are expensive to use.

Transport

1. If it is possible to get by with one car, this will be the biggest cost reduction.

2. Purchase a low-cost and low-mileage used car and drive it until repairs become too expensive.

3. The smaller the car, the more economical to operate. You pay an estimated 25 to 40 percent of the current value of your car each year in total vehicle related costs. Assuming average annual mileage, the cost to run a car per mile ranges from 25 pence to 135 pence.

4. Perform routine maintenance yourself – oil changes, lubrication, etc. Regular maintenance will prolong the life of your car.

Clothing

1. Make a written list of yearly clothing needs. Shop from the list during the sales, or at lower cost clothing shops.

2. Purchase simple basic fashion items that stay in style longer rather than clothes that will soon be out of season.

3. Do not purchase a lot of clothing. Select one or two basic colours for your wardrobe, and buy outfits that you can wear in combination with others.

4.   Purchase home-washable fabrics. Clothes that must be commercially cleaned are expensive to maintain.

Insurance

1.   Select insurance based on your need and budget, check the costs at a number of online sites, making comparisons from at least three major insurance companies.
2.   Raising the insurance excess feature will substantially reduce premiums.
3.   Seek the recommendation of friends for a good insurance agent. A capable agent can save you money. However, make sure you check their rates with those comparable online.

Health

1.   Practice preventive medicine. Your body will stay healthier when you get the proper amount of sleep, exercise and have a balanced diet.
2.   Practice proper oral hygiene for healthy teeth and to reduce dental bills.

Entertainment and recreation

1.   Plan your holidays if you can for the off-peak season and select destinations near home.
2.   Rather than expensive entertainment, seek creative alternatives such as picnics or visits to the local parks.

Five budgeting hints

1.   Reconcile your bank statement with your bank payments and receipts each month.
2.   It is helpful to have a separate savings account where you can deposit the monthly standing order for the bills that do not arise each month. For example, if your annual insurance premium is £480, deposit £40 in this savings account each month. This ensures the money will be available when these payments come due.
3.   We are trained to think how we are paid – either weekly or monthly. To better understand the impact of an expense, calculate the yearly cost. For example, if you spend £4 for lunch each working day, multiply by five days a week by 50 weeks a year. That gives an

annual cost of over £900. Even a coffee a day could cost more than £450 a year. Thinking annually provides a different perspective on those small 'inconsequential' costs.

4. Control your impulse-spending. Impulse-spending ranges from buying expensive items like cars to smaller items such as the latest designer watch. Each time you have the urge to spend for something not planned, post it to an 'impulse list' and pray about the purchase for several days. As you do this, the impulse will often pass.

5. It is wise for husbands and wives to include personal allowances in the budget. Both should be given allowances to spend as they please. Spend within the budget – not a penny more!

Step three – do not stop!

The most common temptation is to stop budgeting. Don't. Many people find it difficult to create a budget by themselves. If you have not yet enrolled in a Crown Financial Ministries small group study, I strongly encourage you to do so. In the small group environment you will be encouraged, yet held accountable to implement biblical financial principles and good budgeting habits.

Remember, a budget is simply a plan for spending your money. It will not work by itself. Every area of your budget should be regularly reviewed to keep a rein on spending. "Any enterprise is built by wise planning, becomes strong through common sense, and profits wonderfully by keeping abreast of the facts" (Proverbs 24:3–4, TLB). There may well be frustrations, but a budget, if properly used, will save you thousands of pounds. It will help you accumulate savings and will help you stay out of debt. More importantly, it will help husbands and wives communicate in an area that is a leading cause of marital conflict.

Commitment

Keep a careful record of all expenditure for 30 days to determine your current situation. After that, plan a budget suited to your income and personal objectives. Put it into effect.

seventeen
Standard of living – how shall we then live?

I was invited to attend the second anniversary of a very special event, the day the Thompsons reached their goal of becoming debt-free. Two years later they were just as grateful for their new freedom and, more importantly, their marriage was growing stronger. Although it had been a struggle for them, and several times they had been on the verge of quitting, the stakes of saving their marriage were too high. They persevered and reached their goal.

> *Let temporal things serve your use, but the eternal be the object of your desire*
>
> **Thomas A Kempis**

Jonathan and Helen were now facing a new challenge; their income now exceeded their expenses. How should they spend the *surplus*? They had major decisions to make. Should they move to a larger home or stay in their present one? Should they purchase a new car? Should they adopt a more expensive lifestyle or continue to save and give more?

The Bible does not dictate one particular standard of living for everyone. However, Scripture contains a number of challenging principles that we should consider when choosing our lifestyle.

Think with an eternal perspective

Nurture an eternal perspective. Our culture and the media implore us to focus on the here and now. Advertisers persuade consumers to gratify themselves today with no thought of tomorrow. Examine the following to understand how brief life is on earth compared with eternity.

Our momentary time on earth is but a dot on the timeline of eternity. Yet we have the opportunity to influence eternity by how we handle money today. We have not only the privilege to lay up treasures for ourselves in heaven but also the opportunity to spend money to influence people for Jesus Christ. Gaining an eternal perspective and eternal values will have a profound effect on your decision making.

Moses is a good example. Let's look at Hebrews 11:24–26: "By faith Moses, when he had grown up, refused to be known as the son of Pharaoh's daughter. He chose to be ill-treated along with the people of God rather than to enjoy the pleasures of sin for a short time. He regarded disgrace for the sake of Christ as of greater value than the treasures of Egypt, because he was looking ahead to his reward."

Moses faced a choice. As Pharaoh's adopted son he could enjoy the lavish lifestyle of royalty, or he could choose to become a Hebrew slave. Because he had an eternal perspective, he chose the latter and was used by the Lord in a remarkable way. We face a similar decision. We can either live with a view toward eternity or live focused on this present world.

Have you ever returned to a place you knew as a child? I once visited a recreational ground where I played when I was 12 years old. I remembered it as a huge field surrounded by fences and a railway line. I was amazed to discover how small it really was! Or do you remember wanting to get something so much you could almost taste it? Yet, today it means almost nothing to you. I think we will experience something similar after we arrive in heaven. Many things that seem so important to us now will fade into insignificance in the light of eternity.

You are a pilgrim

Scripture tells us about our identity and role on earth: First of all, we are citizens of heaven, not earth (Philippians 3:20). Second, we are ambassadors representing Christ on this earth (2 Corinthians 5:20). Third, we are aliens, strangers and pilgrims on this earth (Hebrews 11:13).

Peter wrote "since you call on a Father who judges each man's work impartially, live your lives as strangers here in reverent fear" (1 Peter 1:17).

Later he added "I urge you, as aliens and strangers in the world, to abstain from sinful desires, which war against your soul" (1 Peter 2:11). The pilgrim is a traveller and not a settler – one who is acutely aware that the excessive accumulation of things can only distract from reaching the goal or destination. Material possessions are valuable to a pilgrim only as they facilitate his mission. The pilgrim is a traveller who chooses possessions strategically, regarding most of them as encumbrances that would slow the journey or make it impossible. Of course, many of us become "settlers" in the temporal sense, living in houses and owning furniture and developing businesses. There is nothing wrong with this, but we need to maintain a pilgrim mentality of detachment – the traveller's philosophy of travelling light. Acquire only those possessions that enable you to fulfil God's calling on your life.

Make an effort to live simply

Every possession requires time, attention and often money to maintain it. Too many or the wrong types of possessions can demand so much time, energy or money that they consume our time and maybe harm our relationship with the Lord and others. The quiet, simple life is the best environment to allow us enough time to nurture our relationship with the Lord.

Paul in 1 Thessalonians 4:11–12 counsels: "Make it your ambition to lead a quiet life, to mind your own business and to work with your hands, just as we told you, so that your daily life may win the respect of outsiders and so that you will not be dependent on anybody."

We are at war

"Endure hardship with us like a good soldier of Christ Jesus. No one serving as a soldier gets involved in civilian affairs – he wants to please his commanding officer" (2 Timothy 2:3-4). In the Second World War, people changed their lifestyles radically to help win the war. They rationed the use of strategically important items. They spent less on life's comforts so that the army would be adequately supplied. As soldiers, we should be careful not to become unduly encumbered with the cares of this life.

Recognise the enemy

"For our struggle is not against flesh and blood, but…against the powers of this dark world and against the spiritual forces of evil in the heavenly realms" (Ephesians 6:12). In a war you are going to use your most effective weapon. The devil's mission is to divert us from serving Christ. He frequently accomplishes this by tempting us to serve money and possessions. As we have seen before, money is the primary competitor with Christ for the lordship of our life. "You cannot serve both God and money" (Matthew 6:24).

Serving money is often difficult to recognise because loving money is a 'respectable' sin – people will congratulate you for acquiring the trappings of financial success. Therefore, you should prayerfully examine your relationship with Christ and money.

Spend in a way that pleases the Lord

Prayerfully submit spending decisions to the Lord. Everything we possess is owned by the Lord, and we should spend to please Him and not for a selfish purpose. Seeking the Lord's direction in spending does not mean that we will never spend for anything other than a basic necessity. Recreation, appropriate leisure activities and rest are important. "Since everything God created is good, we should not reject any of it but receive it with thanks" (1 Timothy 4:4, NLT).

Do not waste possessions

"There was a rich man whose manager was accused of wasting his possessions. So he called him in and asked him 'what is this I hear about you? Give an account of your management, because you cannot be manager any longer'" (Luke 16:1–2). Examine yourself. Do you spend money frivolously or waste possessions habitually?

Do not compare yourself to others

Some use comparison to justify spending more than they should. Many have suffered financially because they tried but could not afford to 'keep up with the Joneses.' Someone once said "you can never keep up with the Joneses. Just about the time you catch them, they remortgage their home and go deeper in debt to buy more things!" If you are wealthy, your lifestyle should be based on the conviction that the Lord wants you to have a certain standard of living which is not necessarily dictated by the maximum you can afford.

If only I had more...

Have you ever felt that if only you were in a more prestigious position or had more money, then you could accomplish really significant things for the Lord?

Let's examine two men who lived in Rome and were at different ends of the economic spectrum. Before gladiator contests in the Coliseum, everyone would stand, waiting silently for Caesar. The contests could not begin until he arrived. When Caesar arrived, he was greeted with thunderous shouts of "Hail Caesar!" He had more power, prestige and wealth than anyone else living at that time. He was worshipped as though he were a god.

Elsewhere in Rome was another man in vastly different circumstances. He was in prison, chained to guards. He invested his time praying and writing to his friends. His name was Paul. One man lived in an opulent palace. The other lived in a dingy cell. One had almost unlimited wealth. The other had almost nothing. One was the centre of attention. The other was virtually ignored. Almost 2,000 years later, people around the world recognise which of these two men made the eternally important contribution. They name their children after the prisoner and their salads after the emperor!

Being used by Christ in a significant way has nothing to do with a high position or great riches. It has everything to do with a willingness to allow Christ to become your Lord.

Do not be conformed to this world

Romans 12:2 begins with this command "Do not conform any longer to the pattern of this world, but be transformed by the renewing of your mind. Then you will be able to test and approve what God's will is – his good, pleasing and perfect will."

We live in one of the most affluent cultures the world has ever known. And we are constantly bombarded with costly, manipulative advertising whose purpose is to encourage us to spend money. Advertisers usually stress the importance of image rather than function. For example, car advertisements rarely focus on a car as reliable transportation that is economical to operate; instead, an image of status or sex appeal is projected.

Reflect on the claims of TV commercials. No matter what the product – clothing, deodorants, credit cards, cars, you name it – the message is communicated that the 'fulfilling, beautiful, wrinkle-free life' can be ours if we are willing to buy it. Unfortunately, this media onslaught has influenced all of us to some extent. One commentator put it this way "people buy things they do not need with money they do not have to impress people they do not even like."

The following graph depicts how the artificial, media-generated lifestyle influences our lives. The bottom curve represents our income – what we really can afford to buy. The next curve illustrates how much we actually spend. We make up the difference between our income and spending by the use of debt, which creates slavery, financial pressure and anxiety. The top of the graph demonstrates what advertisers tell us to buy. It is an image-conscious, generally expensive lifestyle that claims to satisfy the human heart's deepest needs. When we want to live this counterfeit, media-induced dream but cannot afford it, we suffer discontentment, envy and coveting.

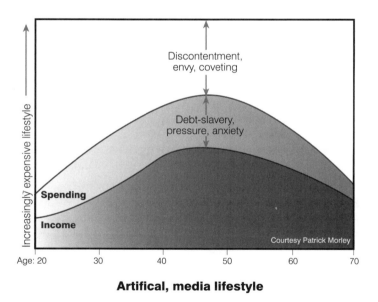

Artifical, media lifestyle

None of us is immune to the lure of this message. Having completed our family budget for the year and decided not to go abroad, I recently found myself looking at a Sunday newspaper travel supplement with a wide

Standard of living – how shall we then live? 17

range of cruising holidays. Every advert seemed to have discounted cruises to every conceivable destination. My wife has always wanted to go to the Norwegian fjords, while I had talked about a cruise in eastern Europe. I was hooked! Then reality took over. Even after the discounts the cost was going to be several thousand pounds. How did that compare to our international travel budget of £nil? About ten minutes after opening the supplement, I jettisoned it onto the pile of other supplements and returned to the sports pages.

Shortly after I received a letter from the manufacturer of my car advising me that I was due to pay £900 for my next year's warranty. I hadn't even thought about including this in my budget. I was in something resembling a state of shock. I contemplated the fact that the car was due for a service and calculated that this was just about to cost me about £1,500. As I drove past the garage I saw a newer model. Instead of 35,000 miles on the clock, this one had only 8,000. For this new car I was only going to have to pay an additional £5,000. We did as we always do in situations like this; we thanked the salesman for his help and returned home. The next day I saw an advert in the newspaper, with the following words, 'Warranty expired or about to expire?' I called the free phone number and received a quote of £500. With a repair bill less than expected I was only £400 over budget, but at least I did not respond to my impulse and spend £5,000 on a new car.

In the space of a week my impulses had been to treat myself to a cruise and to 'save money in the long run' by buying a new car. Not following either of these impulses had saved me £7,500! What is more I had lost the desire for both the new car and the cruise. Interestingly enough with half a day spent cleaning the car inside and out it looks and feels just like a new one!

Did prayer figure in all of this? Yes. Why would I do anything without referring to God – He is after all the owner and I am the steward.

From time to time we all get hooked on something we think we must buy – a car, home, camera, holiday, clothes, you name it. Once hooked, it is easy to rationalise a purchase. Please remember to seek the Lord's guidance and the counsel of a godly person when confronted with a spending decision.

Contrast

Society says: Acquire as many expensive possessions as possible because they are evidence you are a successful, important person.

Scripture says: The excessive accumulation of possessions will distract you from fulfilling God's purpose for your life.

Commitment

I will prayerfully determine what standard of living the Lord wants for me.

eighteen
Perspectives – what's really important

A young Roger Morgan came out of the Appalachian Mountains with the sole purpose of making a fortune. Money became his god, and he became worth millions. Then the stock market crash of 1929 and the Great Depression reduced him to utter poverty. Penniless, he took to the road. One day a friend found him on the Golden Gate Bridge staring down into the waters of the San Francisco Bay, and he suggested they move on. "Leave me alone," Roger replied. "I'm trying to think. There is something more important than money, but I've forgotten what it is." What Roger Morgan forgot, or perhaps never knew, was the scriptural perspective of money. That is what we will explore in this chapter.

> *The futility of riches is stated very plainly in two places: the Bible and the tax return form.*

Money will not bring true happiness

Solomon, the author of Ecclesiastes, had an annual income of more than £15 million. He lived in a palace that took 13 years to build.

He owned 40,000 stalls of horses. He sat on an ivory throne overlaid with gold. He drank from gold cups. The daily menu of his household included one hundred sheep and thirty oxen in addition to fallow deer and fatted fowl.

Obviously, Solomon was in a position to know whether money would bring happiness, and he did not hesitate to say that riches do not bring true happiness: "He who loves money shall never have enough. The foolishness of thinking that wealth brings happiness! The more you have, the more you spend, right up to the limits of your income" (Ecclesiastes 5:10–11, TLB).

In contrast, most people believe you can buy happiness.

If only I had a new car, I would be satisfied. *If only* I lived in that nice house, I would be content. *If only* I had a particular job, I would be happy. The list is endless.

The Bible offers a sharp contrast to this attitude. As someone has said,

Money will buy:
A bed but not sleep;
Books but not brains;
Food but not an appetite;
A house but not a home;
Medicine but not health;
Amusement but not happiness;
A crucifix but not a Saviour.

Is money evil?

Money is not intrinsically evil. It is morally neutral. Money can be used for good, such as supporting missionaries or building hospitals. It also can be used for evil, such as financing illegal drugs and pornography.

Examine 1 Timothy 6:10 carefully: "The *love* of money is a root of all kinds of evil." The Bible does not condemn money itself, only the misuse of or a wrong attitude toward money. Moreover, particularly in the Old Testament, many of the godliest people were among the wealthiest people of the day. Job, Abraham and David were all wealthy, and yet they did not allow wealth to interfere with their relationship with the Lord.

Nevertheless, Scripture warns that riches can destroy a spiritually fruitful life! "The one who received the seed that fell among the thorns is the man who hears the word, but the worries of this life and the deceitfulness of wealth choke it, making it unfruitful" (Matthew 13:22).

Also, it is easy for those who are rich to turn away from God. "When I have brought them into the land flowing with milk and honey, the land I promised on oath to their forefathers, and when they eat their fill and thrive, they will turn to other gods and worship them, rejecting me and breaking my covenant" (Deuteronomy 31:20). Someone once observed, "For every 99 people who can be poor and remain close to Christ, only one can become wealthy and maintain close fellowship with Him." It must be human nature to cling to the Lord when it's obvious that only He can provide our needs. Once people become wealthy, they often take the Lord for granted because they no longer think they have as much need of Him.

Those who love money will never have enough. How meaningless to think that wealth brings true happiness!
Ecclesiastes 5:10, NLT

Will godly people always prosper financially?

Some Christians embrace one of two extremes. Some say if you are really spiritual, you must be poor because wealth and a close relationship with Christ cannot coexist. The second and opposite extreme is the belief that if a Christian has faith, he or she will enjoy uninterrupted financial prosperity.

One end of the spectrum teaches that godliness can occur only in an environment of poverty. However, we already have noted that money is morally neutral and can be used for good or evil. In the Old Testament the Lord extended the reward of abundance to the children of Israel when they were obedient, while the threat of poverty was one of the consequences of disobedience. Deuteronomy 30:15-16 reads, "I set before you today life and prosperity, death and destruction. For I command you today to love the Lord your God, to walk in his ways, and to keep his commands...and the Lord your God will bless you in the land you are entering to possess."

Moreover, Psalm 35:27 reads "let the Lord be magnified, who has pleasure in the prosperity of His servant." We may also pray for prosperity when our relationship with the Lord is healthy: "Beloved, I pray that you may prosper in all things and be in health, just as your soul prospers (3 John 2, NKJV). Let me emphasise that again. The Bible does not say that a godly person *must* live in poverty. A godly person *may* have material resources.

There are those on the other hand who believe all Christians who truly have faith *always* will prosper. This extreme also is in error.

Study the life of Joseph. He is the classic example of a faithful person who experienced both prosperity and poverty. He was born into a prosperous family, then was thrown into a pit and sold into slavery by his jealous brothers. He became a household slave in a wealthy Egyptian's home. His master, Potiphar, promoted Joseph to head the household. Later Joseph made the righteous decision not to commit adultery with Potiphar's wife. Because of that decision, however, he was thrown into prison for years. In God's timing Joseph ultimately was elevated to the position of prime minister of Egypt.

Let's examine four reasons why the godly may not prosper:

1. Violating a scriptural principle

You may be giving generously but acting dishonestly. You may be honest but not properly fulfilling your work responsibilities. You may be a faithful employee but head-over-heels in debt. You may be completely out of debt but not giving.

One of the biggest benefits of this book is that we explore what the entire Bible teaches about money. Those who do not understand all the requirements may neglect critical areas of responsibility. If they suffer financially, they may be confused about the reason for their lack of prosperity.

2. Building godly character

Romans 5:3–4, (NLT) reads "we can rejoice, too, when we run into problems and trials, for we know that they help us develop endurance. And endurance develops strength of character, and character strengthens our confident hope of salvation." An example of the Lord developing character in a people before prospering them is found in Deuteronomy 8:16–18:

He fed you with manna in the wilderness, a food unknown to your ancestors. He did this to humble you and test you for your own good. He did all this so you would never say to yourself, 'I have achieved this wealth with my own strength and energy.' Remember the LORD your God. He is the one who gives you power to be successful, in order to fulfill the covenant he confirmed to your ancestors with an oath.

Deuteronomy 8:16–18 NLT

The Lord knew the children of Israel had to be humbled before they could handle wealth. Our Father knows us better than we know ourselves. In His infinite wisdom He knows exactly how much He can entrust to us at any time without harming our relationship with Him.

3. The mystery of God's sovereignty

Hebrews 11:1–35 lists people who triumphed miraculously by exercising their faith in the living God. But in verse 36 the writer directs our attention abruptly to godly people who lived by faith and gained God's approval, yet experienced poverty. The Lord ultimately chooses how much to entrust to each person. And sometimes we simply can't understand or explain His decisions.

Let's summarise: the Scriptures teach neither the necessity of poverty nor uninterrupted prosperity. What the Bible teaches is the responsibility of being a faithful steward. Please review the following chart and the contrasts between the three perspectives.

	Poverty	Stewardship	Prosperity
Possessions are:	Evil	A responsibility	A right
I work to:	Meet only basic needs	Serve Christ	Become rich
Godly people are:	Poor	Faithful	Wealthy
Ungodly people are:	Wealthy	Unfaithful	Poor
I give:	Because I must	Because I love God	To get
My spending is:	Without gratitude to God	Prayerful and responsible	Carefree and consumptive

4. The rich exploit the poor

A fourth reason why the godly may not prosper is that they are exploited and oppressed, not paid a living wage. Amos 2:6-7 tells us "This is what the Lord says: "For three sins of Israel, even for four, I will not turn back my wrath. They sell the righteous for silver and the needy for a pair of sandals. They trample on the heads of the poor as upon the dust of the ground and deny justice to the oppressed." The prophets repeatedly warn Israel against practicing injustice and hurting the poor.

The Lord's perspective of prosperity

Before we leave the issue of prosperity, it is important to understand that the Lord's perspective of prosperity is contrary to that of our culture. The Lord evaluates true riches based on His spiritual value system. This contrast is stated most clearly in the book of Revelation. The godly poor are rich in God's sight. "I [the Lord] know your tribulation and your poverty (but you are rich)" (Revelation 2:9). Those who are wealthy yet do not enjoy a close relationship with Christ are actually poor. "You say, 'I am rich; I have acquired wealth and do not need a thing.' But you do not realise that you are wretched, pitiful, poor, blind and naked" (Revelation 3:17). True prosperity extends far beyond material possessions. True prosperity is gauged by how well we know Jesus Christ and by how closely we follow Him.

Instructions to those who are rich

Are you rich? Sometimes I feel rich and sometimes I don't. It usually depends on whom I am around. Most of us define a rich person as a person who has more money than we do. But if we compare our living standards to all the people who have lived throughout history or even with the rest of the billions of people living on the earth today, the majority of us who live in this country are rich.

The Lord knew the rich would face serious spiritual danger. So Scripture offers three instructions for "those who are rich in this present world" (1 Timothy 6:17).

1. Do not be conceited

"Command those who are rich in this present world not to be arrogant" (1 Timothy 6:17). Wealth tends to produce pride. For several years, Howard drove two vehicles. The first was an old pickup truck that cost $100. When he drove that truck to the bank drive-in window to cash a cheque, he was humble. Howard knew the cashier was going to double-check his account to make certain that the driver of that truck had sufficient funds to cover the withdrawal. He waited patiently while she checked. When Howard received the money, he was so grateful.

Howard's other vehicle was a well-preserved, second-hand car that was expensive when it was new. When he drove that car to the bank, he appeared to be a different person. He deserved a certain amount of respect. Howard was not quite as patient when the cashier examined his account, and when he received the money, he was not as grateful. Wealth stimulates conceit.

James 1:9–10 addresses this issue: "The brother in humble circumstances ought to take pride in his high position. But the one who is rich should take pride in his low position, because he will pass away like a wild flower."

The poor should be encouraged as children of the King of kings, while the rich are to remain humble because life is short. If you are rich, you need the constant reminder to be humble before the Lord and other people.

2. Put no confidence in your assets

"Command those who are rich in this present world not to be arrogant nor to put their hope in wealth, which is so uncertain, but to put their hope in God, who richly provides us with everything for our enjoyment" (1 Timothy 6:17). For those who have riches, this is unlikely to be easy. In fact this may well present something of a struggle. When I first read *Your Money Counts* (Howard's version), I started to understand the verses regarding God's ownership. All the pieces of my financial jigsaw started to fit together. I had accumulated wealth partly by not drawing anything other than a basic minimum salary. Now I started to see that I had been storing up because God had a plan to engage me to work with Crown Financial Ministries. I hadn't consciously said to the Lord "I know it all belongs to you," but neither had I ever regarded it as mine to spend. Did I get everything right according to Scripture? No. I was over 30 before I recognised the need to tithe. Have I always given generously? No. Have I put my trust in my assets? Yes. Do I put my trust in assets today? Nowhere near as much as I used to. I recently said to Rhoda "well, I came into this world with nothing, and I am prepared to end up with nothing. I am only ever one step from eternity and I do not want my days here to be anything other than full obedience to God."

It is easy to trust in money for money can buy goods and services. It has so much power that it is easy to be fooled into thinking that money supplies our needs and offers security. Money can become our first love. We tend to trust in the seen rather than in the invisible, living God. This is why we need to remind ourselves to walk by faith rather than by sight.

3. Give generously

"Command them to do good, to be rich in good deeds, and to be generous and willing to share. In this way they will lay up treasure for themselves as a firm foundation for the coming age, so that they may take hold of the life that is truly life." (1 Timothy 6:18–19).

As I suggested before, one of the most effective antidotes for the potential disease of loving money is 'setting the finish line.' Determine a maximum amount that you will accumulate. After you have reached your goal, give the rest to build God's kingdom.

Contrast

Society says: Wealth brings happiness and security, and I can use it for my own comfort any way I choose.

Scripture says: True joy is based on my relationship with Christ. In Him alone will I trust. If I am rich, I should be generous and ready to share.

Commitment

I will consistently study the Bible to maintain God's perspective of money and possessions.

nineteen
Summing it all up – let's review

At the beginning of this book we asked why the Bible says so much about money – more than 2,350 verses. The Lord knew that how we handled money would help determine the intimacy of our fellowship with Him. The Lord also wanted to provide us a blueprint for handling money so that we could be faithful in this practical area of life.

There must be the conversion of the heart, the mind and also the purse.

Martin Luther

The fundamental truth for us to understand is that God has retained the responsibilities of ownership of possessions, control of events and provision of needs. As people, we are not designed to shoulder these responsibilities. However, the Lord delegated certain important tasks to us as stewards.

Review the diagram of the wheel and the eight areas of our responsibility.

Financial faithfulness is a journey – do not become discouraged

Applying financial principles from Scripture is a journey that takes time. It's easy to become discouraged. When you finish this book, your finances may not be completely under control. Don't get frustrated. It takes the average person at least a year to apply most of these principles. Again, I want to encourage you to enrol in a Crown Financial Ministries small group study. Visit our website at www.crownuk.org for our contact details. If there is no study group near you, then please register for our small group leader training classes and find out how to start a Crown group in your church. It is an excellent environment to receive encouragement and help in implementing the principles you have read in this book.

Faithfulness in small matters is important

Because of a lack of resources many people become frustrated by their inability to solve their financial problems. Remember, simply be faithful with what you have – whether it is little or much.

Some give up too soon. They abandon the goal of becoming debt free. They stop trying to increase their saving or giving. For them the task seems impossible. And it may be impossible without the Lord's help. Your job is to make a genuine effort, no matter how small it may appear. Then leave the results to God. I love what the Lord said to the prophet Zechariah: "Who despises the day of small things?" (Zechariah 4:10). Don't be discouraged. Be diligent. Be persistent. Be faithful in even the smallest matters.

A good friend once asked me what was the most valuable lesson I had learned from the Crown Financial Ministries small group studies. I have reflected on that question for some time now and think the most valuable thing for me is to know what it means for God to be the owner of everything. Howard Dayton, my mentor in Crown, believes the most valuable lesson has been the realisation that he needed to consistently review Scripture. He told me that he noticed that when preparing for a study group if he invested little time studying Scripture during the previous week, he would discover that he had been moulded ever-so-subtly by the prevailing views of society.

In Romans 12:2 Paul presented this problem and the solution: "Do not conform any longer to the pattern of to this world, but be transformed by the renewing of your mind." The only way for any of us to renew our minds is to expose ourselves to Scripture continually.

The Bible has the answers to the financial problems of the sophisticated twenty-first century. The eternal principles of Scripture are practical in any culture and in any century.

Contentment

At the beginning of this book I said that one of our objectives was that you would learn to be content. 1 Timothy 6:8 issues this challenging statement: "But if we have food and clothing, we will be content with that." Study this passage carefully. It declares that if you have food and covering (clothes and shelter), you should be content. Our culture has restated this verse to read something like this: "if you can afford the finest food to eat, wear the latest fashions, drive the latest upmarket car and live in a beautiful house in the nicest section of town, then you can be happy." Nothing could be further from the truth. There are three elements in learning to be content:

1. Know what God requires of a steward
2. Fulfil those requirements faithfully
3. Trust God to do His part

Once we understand God's responsibilities and we have been faithful in fulfilling our responsibilities as stewards, we can be content. Our loving, heavenly Father will entrust us with the possessions He knows will be best for us at any particular time – whether much or little.

Biblical contentment is not to be equated with laziness, complacency, social insensitivity or apathy. Because we serve the living and dynamic God, Christians should always be improving. Contentment does not exclude properly motivated ambition. We already have discovered that God wants us to work hard. I believe we should have a burning desire to be faithful stewards of the talents and possessions He has entrusted to us. Biblical contentment is an inner peace that accepts what God has chosen for our present vocation, station in life and financial state. Hebrews 13:5 emphasises this: "keep your lives free from the love of money and be content with what you have, because God has said, 'never will I leave you; never will I forsake you.'"

Setting this book free

Some years ago I was listening to a radio programme in Australia. That day the host was talking to an author who was encouraging listeners to 'set their books free.' Intrigued by the concept I listened to the proposal which was to find a shopping arcade, a phone booth or some other public place and leave a book for someone else to read. Searching the Internet, I soon discovered that this is not an unknown practise. I thought of my own bookshelf and decided that passing books on was a good investment to make in the lives of others. Our country has millions who have financial problems and so I encourage you to find someone you know that you think would benefit from reading this book. The first three chapters were specifically written so that they would be an easy read for someone who is not a Christian. As well as for Christians to see the role my own life has played in developing my approach to handling money. If you look at the Crownuk.org website, we have a special offer if you would like to buy this book to give out to others

References

1. Statistics from Credit Action, 2008
2. Charles L. Allen, God's Psychiatry (Old Tappan, NJ: Revell, 1953)
3. David McConaughy, Money, the Acid Test (Philadelphia: Westminster Press 1957), pp 24,25

Plan to complete the Crown Biblical Financial Study

Your Money Counts provides an introduction to Crown's Biblical Financial study course. This ten module programme will help you:

- Avoid the most common financial mistakes
- Get out of debt
- Save, invest and give wisely
- Train your children to manage their finances
- Develop a deeper under standing of work and eternity
- Learn to live free from financial worry

This is a truly amazing course that will help you in many areas of your Christian journey.

This is a module study programme that is designed to last for ten weeks. However, where a church timetable does not permit ten weeks we have included suggestions that embrace a self study and group study so that the course can be completed over four, six or eight weeks.

Self study?
Study the course modules on your own or as a couple – the course adapts to your requirements.

Train to be a Crown Leader?
Register now for our one day Crown leadership classes

Contact Crown at www.crownuk.org

Practical application workbook

The workbook complements the Biblical Financial Study and is integral to our Financially Free series.

The workbook gives practical illustrations based on Matt and Jennifer, a couple who are looking to sort out their finances. Follow this couple through their financial journey, complete the forms they complete and discover a financial system that really works. Includes blank forms and many practical tips.

Use this workbook to look at:

- Your personal financial position
- Your debts, including a snowball plan to get out of debt
- Your planning will be sharpened using our unique '5 budget tests'
- How to cope with unexpected costs and quarterly and annual bills in our 'periodic account' approach
- Look at your insurance cover
- Strategies for preparing or updating a Will
- And much, much more